Mary Starnes

From the Heart

TABLE OF CONTENTS

Acknowledgments

I would like to first thank God for delivering me from my addiction and for putting so many great people in my life.

I would also like to thank my daughter Mary Larson for never giving up hope on me and for loving me and wanting me in her life!

Thank you to the Texas Department of Corrections for allowing Linda Strom and those of Discipleship Unlimited to open the faith based dorms within the prison walls, as I have no doubt that I would not have changed my life if it had not been for the love and devotion of Linda Strom and the many wonderful volunteers, that worked with us and loved us and taught us about God and so much more. Linda Strom, I love you sooo much!!!

I would like to thank my friends, The Sister Chicks For Christ - Ty Washington, Merry Fuller and DeAnne Barber- who have been there through the good times and the bad and who have been an endless source of strength and encouragement to me.

I would like to thank my Parole Officer Mrs. Catherine Dutch, who has had faith in me from the beginning and who has been full of encouragement and kindness from the start! There should be more parole officers like you!

I would also like to give a special thanks to my current boss Mrs. Elvira Medina who gave me a chance to work through a company when no one else would and who has been so kind and helpful to me.

To Catherine Arredondo and her husband Chris for being such good friends and helping us when we lost our house. To my church family at Rosen Heights Baptist Church and its pastor, Inavi Jimo and his wife, who welcomed my husband and me with open arms and has helped us numerous times.

And last-but-not-least, to my husband Larry Starnes for loving me and putting up with me for the last 12 + years and for rescuing me from my past. I love you baby, and you are a real blessing to me!

I also owe a special thanks to a very special lady, Joyce Delaney, without whom I would not have learned to have faith in myself and my ability to grow and do better. She was such a great source of faith, love, hope and comfort both during the time I was in prison and after I was released from prison. She taught me how to love myself for the first time in my life! Thank you, Joyce, you will always have a special place in my heart! God bless you!

Introduction

<u>Through A Child's Eye</u>

I sometimes wish I could see the world through a child's eyes
And I bet if I could I would get a big surprise
I sometimes wish I could see the world through a child's eyes
For they see things that we don't realize.
The older people can learn from the younger generation
And you know, I sometimes look at them with admiration.
So someday, why not ask your child for his or her suggestion
And you may just find the answer to your question...

I wrote this poem because I feel as if my childhood was stolen from me before it ever began. I don't think that I ever really saw the world through a child's eyes, as my innocence was stolen at a young age. I was forced to grow up way too early and way too fast because of the abuses I suffered from my father and even in some ways from my mother. Especially in today's world, I don't feel that adults listen to their children when they should. Maybe they think they hear what is being said, but do they really HEAR what is being said?

Child abuse, and children being murdered by their own parents, and children killing their parents is too common in today's world. When I was growing up I hated God, as I could not understand how there could possibly be a loving and caring God who would allow such bad things to happen to a child. I would ask myself, how could it be that there is a loving God, yet an innocent child is allowed to go through so much pain and sorrow? It took years for me to realize that it was not "God who ALLOWED bad things to happen to me", but that God gave us free will and we do things of our free will.

In retrospect, I would not change anything in my life, because I can use my past pain and sorrows for the glory of God in helping those who suffer now. I sincerely pray that my book will be a way to help those who are lost to God, to help them see that the only way that they can change their lives and live in peace, is to find the Lord - and in doing so find peace in their lives. Does that mean that they will not suffer or go through trials and tribulations in their lives? Absolutely not. We are allowed to go through trials and tribulations, because God knows it will work to shape us, to help us **grow** through our life experiences, and become stronger both mentally and spiritually!

As a child, I did not realize that God was with me through everything that I went through and that He helped me to survive. Had God not been with me, though I did not know it at the time, I would never have made it through half the things I did survive. If you are reading my book, I pray that it will help to give you peace of mind, hope and a desire to change your life.

This is a photo taken of me while I was in my addiction

This is a photo of me since living my life through Christ!

Chapter One: Broken Beginnings

From a child who had been abused and mistreated all her life,
To an adult who lived in sadness and so much strife.
Going from being all alone without acceptance or love
and not wanting to live,
To someone who learned to overcome the past
and learned how to forgive.
There didn't seem to be any hope for a better future,
How can she go on, what else will she have to endure?
But then someone brought God into her life
And showed her there was hope,
They showed her the way to live and love
and they gave her the skills to cope.

My life ended before it ever really began. My father molested me at a young age, and over time he convinced me that I was ugly and worthless and would never amount to anything. My mother was, as good of a mother as she could be, as she herself had been raised by my tyrant father; she was 16 when she got together with my father. He taught her to loathe herself and tore her self-esteem down to nothing. He convinced her that she was nothing without him and that no one else would want her if he were to leave. He told her that this was because she had four kids, was fat and ugly, and no one would want to raise four kids by another man.

My oldest sister was a year older than I; she was mean and vicious and full of hate, just like my father. My younger brother by two years was loving, caring, kind and did not have a mean bone in his body. It was hard to provoke him into any kind of violence or a fight. He was a gentle soul. My next younger brother by three years had to be a fighter to survive, as not only was he the youngest of us four children, but he was the smallest as well.

My father was a tall, slim Logger whose purpose in life was to work, drink, and come home to terrify and abuse his wife and children. He would go to the bar after work and get drunk and come home to sleep it off. My father moved us to the country and said that it was to keep us kids out of trouble. I have always felt that he wanted my mother in the country, so he could cheat on her without the fear of getting caught, and so no one would see the abuse that he was inflicting on all of us.

My father painted me as a troubled child who was a liar and a thief, and a big "drama mama". Therefore, no one would listen to me if I tried to tell anyone of the abuse that I suffered at his hands. I remember a time when my sister stole some jewelry from a neighbor and blamed it on me because the neighbor wanted me to replace my sister as her babysitter. You see, the neighbor believed me to be more responsible than my sister and thought I would be the better choice. When the neighbor told my parents that she was missing some jewelry, my father waited until she left and then he asked me where the jewelry was. I told him that I did not know anything about the theft of her jewelry, but he did not believe me. He took me outside and had a clamp in his hands, and he put my hand on a tree stump then took an axe and threatened to cut my fingers off, if I did not admit that I had stolen the jewelry. He held the axe over his shoulder as if he was going to really chop off my fingers, and I was afraid for my safety, so I told my father that I had stolen the jewelry. That was only one of many times that I was abused by him.

When my father punished us, he would beat us on our bare skin with a belt. Whenever we got into trouble, we were always punished more than once. First, we got punished by my mother and when my father got home, we were punished again. I remember, when I knew I was going to get into trouble with my father, I would go to bed early thinking that he would not wake me up to punish me. But how wrong I was; he would jerk me out of bed out of a dead sleep and start yelling and beating me!

Not only was I abused at home, but I was mistreated on the school bus and at school as well. The other kids would pull my hair, spit on me, spit wads at me, stick my head in a dirty toilet or a trash can, and try to shove me into a locker and close the door. I began to wonder what was wrong with me; why everyone felt it necessary to embarrass and humiliate me at school, and why my father always felt the need to beat on me. I remember, I used to fantasize that I was adopted. I refused to dress down at Physical Education class as I did not want anyone to see all the bruises on my body. I was the only child probably in the history of the school to flunk PE. I started to hate school so much that I would go through extremes to not have to go to school. I once plucked out all my upper eyelashes on both eyes on my way to school. My mother drove us to school that day, as she had errands to run and she was going in that direction. No one in the car even realized what I had been doing in the back seat. The moment that I stepped into the classroom, the teacher noticed my red eyes all puffed up and sent me directly into the nurse's office. The school nurse called my mother instantly and told her that I would have to go to a dermatologist and see what caused my eyelashes to fall out. No one even noticed that ONLY the top lashes were missing or that I was perfectly fine when I got into the car. I had to stay home till my eyelashes grew back but it did not stop the homework; my sister was given my homework and was responsible to make sure that it got back to the teacher.

Sadly, that was not the only time that my mother did not notice that there was something wrong with her daughter. By the time I was 8 years old, I had been raped and or molested 8 times. The first man who molested me, after my father, lived in the country near us. I had befriended a lady who lived in the country, as she paid attention to me and talked nice to me and did things with me. It was a great feeling to have someone show me attention in a positive way. Her brother-in-law thought that I was a cute little girl, and I had decided that bad attention was better than no attention at all and besides, there was no way that I could fight him off and no one would believe me anyway, so I gave in to his desires. I felt that since my father had already molested me why would one more matter?

When my mother did finally get tired of my father, because she found out that he had cheated on her (which she had always suspected), she kicked him out of the house. The problem was, my mother had not worked a day in her life, and she did not have any marketable skills. How was she going to take care of four kids and herself with no income? At the time, she did not know anything about welfare and food stamps. A lady who lived at the bottom of the hill, worked in a warehouse and she told my mother that she could get her a job there, and her kids could make sure that we got on the bus to school. My mother took the job, so she would have the means to take care of her children. The lady had 3 girls and a boy, all older than us kids were. Since we were the most unpopular kids in school, it did not make her kids happy to have to be seen with us.

In the afternoons, her teenage son oversaw taking us home. One day on the way home, he stopped halfway between our house and his, and he told my siblings to wait in the truck as he had something that he wanted to show me. He took me into the woods and told me that we were going to play a game, and if I told anyone he would kill all of us. He then molested me, and he urinated all over my dress. Again, my mother did not even know that there was anything wrong with me and I was too afraid to tell.

One day, another of my mother's friend and her husband convinced my mother to allow me to spend a weekend with them, so she could have a break. She and her husband thought it would be cool to see how an 8-year-old would act high on pot, so they got me stoned. I got so stoned that I sat staring at the wall glassy eyed, and I found a stone frog and picked it up, and I started petting it and saying over and over "nice little froggy, nice little froggy". They began to worry after several hours that I would not snap out of it before my mother came to get me. Lucky for them, I did snap out of it before my mother arrived.

I guess my mother got tired of being alone, and my father must have gotten bored with his girlfriends, and they ended up getting back together and it was back to the same old abuse again in no time. I had decided at this point that I was tired of being mistreated at home and at school and I began running away from home. My mother made it a condition of his coming back home that we move back into town, as she did not like having to be stuck in the country all alone. That was fine with me, it made it easier for me to run away.

One day when I was supposed to be leaving for school, I took off down the road and started hitching a ride out of town to Medford where I could hitch a ride to Modesto, California. You see, I had made a friend at school whose mother was a single parent and an alcoholic, and she had told her mother that I was getting abused at home and that she wanted me to go with them to California. Her mother said that I could go, but I would have to find my own way there, as she did not want to get into trouble for kidnapping or harboring a runaway. I don't know if the people I got rides with believed my stories about why I was hitching rides to California or if they just did not care? You see, most of the people I got rides from were horny truck drivers and all they cared about was having sex with me.

One night when I was only about 5 miles from my destination, I got a ride from a guy in a small Mazda pickup and the guy waited until we got close to an orchard, then he stuck a knife to my throat and told me to take my clothes off. He told me that if I tried to get away or if I made any loud noises that he would kill me. He tied me to a tree where he started to torture me by cutting me on my chest, then inserting the metal end of a screwdriver into my rectum and a lit cigarette into my vagina. He then cut me loose and began raping me. While all of this was happening to me, I just stared into the night sky with tears running down my face as I begged God to let me die! I was already tired of life and the way I got treated in life. I had nothing and no one who loved me, I was all alone in the big cruel world and I just wanted it all to end.

When he was done, he told me that he was going to let me go but that if he caught me looking at his truck or his license plate, then he would come back and kill me. He took all of my clothes and my backpack and threw them throughout the orchard, then he took off leaving me alive in the orchard with no clothes on, cold, scared and all alone. Once he was gone, I went through the orchard looking for my clothes and backpack. It was now almost daylight, so I did not have much time to decide what I was going to do. I waited in the orchard till it was daylight so that I could try to get another ride to my friend's house. When her mother opened the door and saw the condition that I was in, she refused to let me in, as her mother was afraid that she would get blamed for what had happened to me.

My friend's mother called the police and said that there was a young female child outside of her house who looked like she had been beaten badly. The police arrived shortly after my friend's mother called them, and they picked me up and took me to the hospital to get checked out. The doctor told them that I had been tortured and beaten and that there was evidence that I was raped.

Children's Services came for me at the hospital, and I ended up staying at a social workers house for the weekend, so that I would not have to spend the weekend in Juvenile Hall. She was a very nice black lady, but her daughters were mean and began mistreating me. So, I stole some money from a family member's purse, and I took off again. Once again, the police found me and immediately sent me home to my parents. It wasn't long after I returned home, that the abuse began again and this time I called CPS to report it. My mother told them that I was trouble, and she and my father did not want to be responsible for me anymore.

Chapter Two: Into The System

The System

I was stuck in the system for the majority of my life
You see, no one loved me, I was all alone in this world full of pain and strife
In all, I went through the system four different times because of my addiction,
which in itself was the worst of my crimes
It's sad that it didn't bother me to be in the system,
but I guess it's because I had been there so many times
The last time I was in the system, I was placed in a faith-based dorm
The volunteers were so loving, and kind and they were warm

They taught me about the Lord and how very much he loved me
They taught me how to let go of my anger and pain;
taught me to ask him to set me free
For the first time in my life I embrace the future and welcome whatever it brings
Because I know God will take care of me and will guide me through all things

It was decided that I would be sent to a co-ed place called Timmons Shelter home for troubled youth until it could be decided what my fate would be. At Timmons, we had chores, counseling, and we had to go to school. Our route to school took us past the dog shelter, where I saw my dear sweet dog Trixie sitting there looking sad and all alone. My parents had gotten rid of her as they didn't want any memories of me around. I asked the lady in the dog pound about her fate and she said that she was scheduled to be put down because she was too old and no one wanted an old dog. It broke my heart and I asked the staff if there was any way that I could keep her with me at the shelter home. They said that they were sorry, but pets were not allowed at the shelter. It was so hard for me to imagine my Trixie being put to death! At that moment, I hated my parents more than I had ever hated them before. Trixie was always there for me when I was in pain and hurting after one of my father's beatings. I thought of Trixie and how scared she must have been and how alone she was, and I thought to myself that she was as bad off as I was, all alone, unwanted and hurting.

The next day on the way to school, I bent down to pet her, and I stole the collar from around her neck. I hugged her and said goodbye to her with tears running down the side of my face. I knew that my father was mean and cruel enough to do this to my dog, but I could not believe that my mother would allow this to happen to my dog. After school, I went to my room at the shelter home and I closed the door and cried my eyes out. I was hurt and angry, and I hated my parents and the world.

That night, I took an eyeshadow pencil and wrote "you're going to die bitch" on my bedroom window, then I laid in my bed and started screaming! The counselors came running and asked me what was wrong, and I showed them what was on the window. Somehow, they guessed that I had done it myself, and they began to believe that I was more troubled than they had originally thought.

As a whole, the home really wasn't a bad place to be. I even had a room of my own for the first time in my life. We were paid for our chores and we had to walk two buildings down the road to go to school. The staff were very nice, and on the weekends if we were on our best behavior, we were treated to going to the movies and sometimes we got together with other "troubled youth" from a place called Star Gulch Ranch, which was in the country and was one step away from reform school. We would play basketball and visit with one another.

After the eyeshadow pencil incident, it was decided that I needed to be taken to Star Gulch, as they were better equipped to deal with youth who were as damaged and troubled as I was. By this time, I was 11 years old and they had no idea what to do with me. Other than running away from home (which back then was considered breaking a law), I had not broken any laws, but I was a troubled kid and I was heading in the wrong direction. It was then that CPS decided to send me to that co-ed place called Star Gulch Ranch. When CPS came to get me to take me to the ranch, they brought my mother with them and told me where I was going, and they told me to make the best of it because it was my last chance before being taken to reform school. They assured me that the reform school named Hillcrest, was not a place where I wanted to be. I begged my mother not to allow them to send me to Star Gulch, with tears running down my face and urgency in my voice, but my mother said that it was for my own good that I go.

When we arrived at Star Gulch Ranch, my mother took out my suitcase and the social worker told me to follow them to this double wide trailer. As I walked, I looked around the property and I noticed a huge building to one side and another on the opposite side of it. There was a dome shaped building to the left of the trailer, and between the trailer and the two buildings was a school house. Down from the dome was another building that was the chow hall. There were trees everywhere and a creek down below the trailer. The dome shaped building was a game room, and the two buildings by the schoolhouse and the trailer were dorms. One was a dorm for girls and the other was for boys. The trailer served as an office where all the counselors held sessions and one room was the director's office.

I was led into the director's office and introduced to her. She was a kind, grandmotherly type and she introduced herself and then began to tell me what would be expected of me while I was there. I was then taken to the front of the trailer and introduced to the counselors who would be in charge of me, and who would explain to me in detail what would be expected of me. There was a lady from CPS that was a ranch counselor and she was kind, with long brown hair and a soft, kind voice; and she smoked long brown cigarettes. She gave me my dorm assignment and told me that if I did well and graduated from the program that I could go back home. But if I did not make it there that I would have to go to Hillcrest. I was introduced to a couple of other counselors who told me the rules and told me that I would have to follow them to the fullest.

There was a married couple that worked there as counselors who I became very close to, and then an older, very kind man who would come to mean a lot to me as well. I would have to go to school, do my share of the chores for which I would be paid, and go to all groups. One of the staff members (the older, kind man) said that as part of the intake process, I would be required to see a special movie, then I would be asked to discuss the movie later, so I needed to pay close attention to the movie. It turned out to be a movie about a little girl who had been molested! I lost it and that is when CPS began to suspect that my father had molested me. I took off running outside and was crying uncontrollably as I ran down to the creek.

The male counselor waited awhile before he went to check on me, as he wanted to give me a chance to come to terms with what I had seen in the movie. When he found me, he asked me if I was okay? I told him that I was fine and did not want to talk about the stupid movie. He respected my wishes and did not force me to talk to him about the movie, but he did report it to the director who then discussed it with the CPS worker. The next day, I was pulled out of the classroom by a female counselor and she wanted to discuss the movie I saw the day before. I would never admit to her or anyone else that my father had molested me as I felt shame and disgust, and I knew that everyone would think that I was just lying and trying to make trouble. I told her that I was just an over emotional kid and that cried at movies. They let it go, but they did not believe that there was nothing to my show of emotions.

After about three months of being there, I and five other kids decided to run away from Star Gulch Ranch. I don't know why I ran away, because the staff there was kind to me, and it really wasn't a bad place to be. I guess it was because I wanted to fit in or maybe it is because I was tired of being there, who knows why? As I said before, it was far out into the country (I think it was about 15 or 20 miles out of town), so it took a long time for us to get to town. Eventually, we were caught and taken back to the ranch. It was a strict rule that if you run away from the ranch that you would be kicked out of the program. I feared that I had really done it this time, I just knew that I was going to be sent to

Hillcrest, and I was probably going to get beat up there. I am not sure why, but they decided to give me another chance. I guess the director saw something in me or she had high hopes for me or perhaps it was a part of God's plan for me and my future...?

There was a boy who I became interested in and we were together until it was time for me to leave. He was a very sweet and kind boy and he made me feel special and cared for and pretty. Once while I was at Star Gulch Ranch, we all as a group, made a totem pole which had carvings of Rock-N-Roll groups and at the top of the pole was an eagle for the band The Eagles. It had AC/DC, Van Halen, and many other such cool groups on it. The Medford Mail Tribune sent a reporter out to the ranch to do a story about our totem pole which I thought was cool! It was a lot of fun to make the totem pole and to help put it in the ground. In a way, the people at Star Gulch had become more of a family to me then I had ever had before.

Finally, it came time for me to leave the ranch, as I had successfully completed the program to their satisfaction. I was sad, nervous and scared because I did not want to go back home. In fact, I begged them to allow me to stay there because though I had changed, I knew that the circumstances at home and the people at home had not! Though the director was sympathetic to my dilemma, it was her job to reassure me that it would be okay! I knew better because I knew that my father would never change. I went through sort of a transformation at the ranch, but my family had not gone through counseling so though I was different, they were the same. My mother showed up to my graduation ceremony and dinner (of course my father did not come) and my mother, perhaps for the first time in my life, told me that she was proud of me!

Chapter Three: Among The Wolves

What is the life of a child, how is it supposed to be?
Isn't it supposed to be full of love and laughter,
Can someone out there please tell me.
A child should not have to live a life of anger and
bitterness or be taught to live in fear,
Their lives should start out being pure, full of happiness
and cheer.
I always wondered what a normal childhood is supposed to
be like in a normal family,
Because the childhood I lived was full of sadness and I was
always lonely.

We went home and as I expected, nothing at all had changed. It was not long before my father started beating and mistreating me again, and I was not going to go through that again. Therefore, once again I put on my running shoes and took off to California with no money, nowhere to arrive to, and no idea what I was going to do. I just knew that ANYWHERE had to be better than home. I found my friend who I was going to go stay with at the time I was raped and beaten in the orchard. At this point I was 11 years old and no better off than when I was eight years old.

I went through a lot before I found her. I had no money, no food, and nowhere to stay. I ended up having to sleep with men for a motel room to sleep in, food to eat, and to be able to stay clean. It is sad that men were so willing to have sex with a child. I slept at times in junk yards and in abandoned cars or vacant houses.

I went hungry many times because no matter how hungry I got, I could not bring myself to steal, and I could not bring myself to beg. I guess you could call it pride? Funny isn't it, I had too much pride to beg but not too much pride to sell my body for food and a warm place to lay my head. I began to hate myself even more because I used my body as a means to survive, much as a prostitute does, so I guess you could say that I was a child prostitute.

I found a farmer who was willing to allow me to work in the grape orchard picking grape leaves along with the Mexican people for 17 cents a pound. We had to make sure that the leaves did not have holes in them, were not too big and not too small, and were not too brown. When we had a pound, we were given a ticket and at the end of the week, we turned in our tickets for our pay. The only reason why they were so willing to allow me to work there, is for the same reason they allowed the Mexican people to work without permission, it was cheaper to allow it because we worked for less pay. When I found my friend, I stopped working in the field, and she would introduce me to old men who would pay us to allow them to touch our breasts and play with the rest of our bodies.

Before I knew it, I was 12 years old in actual age, but about 20 years old in life. My friend convinced me that I should start doing drugs so that I could deal with what I had to do to survive. She also said that I would no longer have bad dreams about my past, nor even think about the past. That sounded good to me, not having to think about my past or having to deal with what I had to do to survive.

At first, it was just a little bit of cocaine and speed that I was snorting... than anything else that I could get my hands on that would send me into oblivion. By the time I was 13 years old, I was putting a needle in my arm. I had to have someone do it for me because I didn't ever learn how to inject myself. I guess that it was a good thing that I did not know how to inject myself, as my addiction would have been much worse. I had to pay other addicts to inject me with the dope, so I had to work even harder to make more money, so I could pay someone to give me my injection. I stayed this way for 2 years, at which time I decided to go back home to Oregon.

I am not sure why I wanted to go back to that place which was so full of bad memories, but nonetheless, I had the urge to go. So, I stuck out my thumb and I started hitching rides back to Oregon, and I met someone who I liked at a party. He was a Mexican guy called Botchie. We were together for a year when he asked me to marry him. I was only 16 years old at the time, and the legal age to get married was 18 without a parent signing the papers. So, I went to my parents and I asked them to sign the papers, and they wouldn't do it. So, Botchie and I told his step mother, and she said that I could go to court and prove that I was able to care for myself; that I could get emancipated which meant by law that I was a legal adult and thus I could get married.

I went to court and provided the proof that I needed to become emancipated. A month later, he and I were married. I was happy, as I thought that I had finally found someone who loved me, and I would prove that my father was wrong - I was loveable! Unfortunately, a few months later I began to feel that my father was right, maybe no one would ever truly love me. A month after we were married, Botchie asked me to help him become an American Citizen, so he would not have to live in fear that he would be taken back to Mexico and away from me. Of course, I was only too willing to do so, as I did not want the man that I loved to be deported.

Then one day I caught him kissing his step sister! When I interrupted them, he quickly explained that he was in love with her, but he needed me as she was too young to marry. I was so hurt and angry over his betrayal, that I got a .38 revolver and started chasing him through the orchard where his father worked, and where we lived. Thank God I couldn't hit the bright side of a barn and missed him shot after shot.

Later that day, I called Immigration to come pick him up and take him back to Mexico. I guess I felt that if I could not have him and his love, she would not have him or his love either! Botchie told them that they could not take him as he was married to an American Citizen. They asked him, "Who do you think called us?". As soon as the Immigration officials picked him up, I loaded his car full of stuff that could be sold including guns, jewelry, and anything else of value that I could find, and I took it and sold all of it. His parents called the police and tried to get me arrested, but they told his parents that since I was married to him, I had as much right to his property as he did so there was nothing that they could do about it.

By now I was almost 18 years old, with no high school diploma and no marketable job skills and all alone once again. I went to a party and I met this guy named Saul. We partied all night long and the next morning, he had to go to work and said that after work he would take me wherever I wanted to go. While I was waiting in a friend's trailer for him to take me home, Jesse came by to see him and introduced himself to me. Since I was still high from the drugs that we had done the night before, in conjunction with the large amount of alcohol that we consumed, I was still not feeling well. Jesse asked if I was Saul's girlfriend, and I laughed and said that I had just met him the night before.

Jesse talked me out of my clothes and enticed me with some crank (Methamphetamines). Once we were done having sex, he said that he would give me a ride home. I remember that day as if it were just yesterday. I was wearing a blue jean skirt (mini skirt), a pair of knee-high boots, a halter top, and a black cowboy hat that Jesse hand placed on my head. Jesse asked me to allow him to buy me something to eat to help me feel better. Then he talked me into allowing him to take me to a park to get some fresh air. He was a great sweet- talker, so great in fact that he not only talked me into going to the park with him, but also into spending the night with him and another, and another, and another.

Before I even realized it, I was now his live-in girlfriend. We were staying in a small camp trailer on a horse ranch, and he spoiled me rotten, but he was a very controlling man. He made me feel desirable and special like no one else ever had! I walked around with my head held high thinking that I was special that a man like Jesse wanted me! We never ate at home; we always went out to eat at some nice restaurant. One day, while he was at work, I got a call from a woman who said that she needed to talk to Jesse. I asked her who she was and what she wanted with him. She again asked where he was, so I told her that he was at work. She told me to tell Jesse that she wanted to deal for him and that if he said no that she would turn him into the cops.

I did not understand... was Jesse a drug dealer? I never saw him with a large amount of drugs and he was always by my side, and he worked all day on the ranch, so how could it even be possible for him to be a drug dealer? I gave Jesse the message when he got home from work and I asked him what she meant. He told me not to worry about it, that he would take care of it himself. The next thing I knew, I was going for a ride with Jesse and his friend Saul. It was a late summer night and I was in the van with Jesse, and we were going to a park in Medford to meet with Saul and Maria, the lady who had called and left the message for Jesse. Maria got into the car with Saul and we were apparently all going for a ride somewhere. I asked Jesse where we were going, and he told me that we were going to spend a couple of hours out at Agate Lake in Eagle Point. I did not know at the time, but it would be the last time I would see Maria alive.

Once we arrived at the lake, Jesse told me to go wait by the van for a moment because he needed to go speak privately to Maria. Saul came up behind me and held a .38 revolver to my head and he said for me to watch very carefully at what happens to people who either threaten or betray Jesse. He told me to watch, learn, and keep my mouth shut. I heard Jesse tell Maria that he was going to give her a chance to run for her life. But instead, he shot her in the head and after she was dead, Jesse had sex with her! I could not believe what I was seeing with my own eyes! I was scared to death; more fear ran through me than I had ever felt in my entire life. Though I was scared out of my wits, I had to remain calm and keep my cool if I had any hope of making it out of this situation alive. Saul was still holding the .38 to my head while I was made to watch. After Jesse was done - He, Saul and I went to a gas station where a friend of his worked, and his friend took the tires off of the car and the van and threw them into a pile of tires that were going to be disposed of the next morning. Afterwards, Jesse and I drove to an orchard near where he worked, and Jesse placed the pistol that he used to kill Maria with inside of the bag and he threw it up in the tree. Then we drove to the trailer and Jesse said that he was tired and wanted to go to sleep. After he turned out the lights, whether it was real or imagined, I started hearing noises in the dark and I was afraid that he would kill me next, as I was the only witness to the murder besides Saul - who was an old trusted friend who had somehow proven his loyalty to Jesse long ago. I suddenly felt as though I had become a disposable girlfriend.

Once he left for work the next morning, I started searching through the trailer to see what I could find out about this man who I thought was so kind and gentle.... What I found was disturbing to say the least. I found a handkerchief under the small stove in the trailer and it had a huge rock of cocaine in it! Not only did I find a big rock of cocaine, but I also found a cop's badge, so either he was a bad cop, or the badge was a fake and at the time I was not sure which and did not know which would be worse for me! I then decided, that after the rough night that I had had and the stuff that I had found in the trailer, that it was time for me to get the Hell out of there and fast! There was no time to waste, though I was not even sure what I was going to do or where I was going to go. When Jesse came back for lunch, I told him that I wanted to go visit my mother as she called and wanted me to meet her for lunch. I took his van (the van that we were in the night before), and I went to my mother's house, and she was not there. I tried to call her on the cell phone, but she did not answer.

So, I headed down the freeway without a clue where I was going to go or what I was going to do. I spotted my mother's friend Joan's car going down the freeway, and I was frantically honking the horn to get her attention, so that I could see if she knew where my mother was. My mother was in the car with Joan and they were on their way to California, which was just beyond the Oregon border. I told her that I desperately needed her help. She asked me, "what did you do now?" I told her that it was not what I did, but what Jesse did. I told her that I could not tell her what Jesse had done as it could put her in danger. She said that if I did not tell her what Jesse did then she would not help me. I made her promise that if I told her, that she would and could not tell anyone, as it could get us all killed. I wanted to make sure that she understood the seriousness of the information that I was about to give her. So, I told her how things started and about Jesse killing Maria. I told her where he had killed Maria and how I was terrified. She told me that she would help me and for me just to go upstairs and take a shower. As soon as I went upstairs to take a shower, that I hoped would relax me, she got on the phone with the police and old them everything that I had told her.

Then sent some cops to the lake and found Maria's body and called it into the station. When I came downstairs, I came face to face with the police and they were there to pick me up as a material witness! They put me in a jail cell to await Jesse's trial (once they were able to catch him that is). Turned out, they wanted my help with catching him as well.

They had me go with them in a police car, to where Jesse and I had been living, so they could see if he was at home. He was not home, so we started to head to a couple of other places where Jesse may be, and I spotted Jesse's van going down the road heading to our house. I started yelling, "That's him, that's him". They made a quick U-turn and called to the other cars that were in the area, and they made him pull over, and I ducked down so he could not see me in the police car. A lot of police were out of their cars with rifles pulled and aimed at him, as they ordered him to get slowly out of the car. The police then took me back to jail and put me back in the cell, where I felt as though I was under arrest.

I utilized my time in jail by attempting to get my GED. I did get my GED while I was there though my score was not the greatest. After I finished with my GED, I became anxious and bored, and I felt as though I was losing it! I was not allowed to have a cellmate as they were afraid that somehow it would get to Jesse that I was there before the trial, so I was forced day-after-long-day to stay in that jail cell all alone. After a couple of weeks, I finally told the guard that I needed to speak to someone about my situation, and I needed to get out of this place. They had me get in touch with an aunt of mine that lived out of state, to see if she would allow me to stay with her until it was time for me to testify, and they would pay her to allow me and an undercover officer to stay at their house. My aunt and uncle agreed to allow us to stay at their house. The officer and I traveled in an unmarked car from Oregon to Idaho until we reached my family's house.

We were there I think a couple of days when I got a call saying, "We know where you are bitch, and we are coming for you"! I think I came as close to being as scared as I was when this whole mess started. I panicked, and I found the officers car keys and some travelers checks, and I took off like a bat out of Hell down the road. It was a gravel road, so I got to thinking that I better slow down before I spin out. As I applied pressure to the breaks, I began to spin out of control and went into a spin and then flipped a couple of times, when the car finally rolled up against a haystack. I didn't (by the grace of God and some miracle) have a scratch on me. I got out of the car and I started walking, until I reach a motel where I got a room using a forged travelers check. Before I knew it, the police had found me and took me to the county jail, until I could be flown back to Oregon and put back in the county jail until Jesse's trial.

My mom came to see me when I was in jail; but she only came to see me as she wanted me to release some money to her, as she knew that they were putting money on my books for commissary. As soon as she got the money, she left! They eventually let Jesse go for insufficient evidence (or so they said, but I think that they were trying to catch him with something else.) A few months later, they pulled him over with a van full of illegal weapons and drugs and lots of money. They told me to pick out my new name and they took me to Salt Lake City, Utah.

They gave me some money, put me up in a hotel, and told me that my handler would come and get me in a couple of days with my new ID and the information that I would need to know to start my new life. I was not supposed to contact anyone in my family or in my past, but after my handler left the motel room, I went shopping with the money that he had left me, and I went to a jewelry store and bought my mother a mother's ring with authentic stones and a rabbit fur coat. I met a lady who I thought was nice and she talked me into staying with her. I had to contact my handler and let him know that I was not going anywhere and that I wanted to keep my name and stay where I was. He asked my new friend if she was sure she wanted me to be around her and her kids when it could put them at risk. She said that she was sure that no one would find me there. Later, I wished I would have gone through the witness protection program, as things didn't work out between she and I, and I was once again alone and in the streets with nothing. After that, I went all over the country hitching rides and going from state to state, and I went to California again where I ended up at a drug dealer's house.

Chapter Four: Stuck In Insanity

Stuck in Insanity

What causes someone's life to spin so far out of control and drift into darkness
What makes them turn to drugs and turn their lives into such a mess
What caused them so much pain and sorrow that they no longer care about life
That they would prefer living in a world full of loneliness and strife
What happened to these people to turn them into addicts believing they had no worth
Isn't it sad to know that there is so much darkness on this earth?
What could have happened to change these lost souls so thoroughly
What can we do to help them, maybe love them unconditionally?

While I was there, the house was raided by the police. The dealer's old lady threw a hypodermic needle full of dope in my purse, so off I went to jail for Possession of a Controlled Substance. I was there for three weeks when they decided to make me a Trustee. My job was to wash police cars and I did it unsupervised. One day, instead of going back to the jail for lunch, I decided that I was going to run off from the job. We were allowed to have up to $10 in change at a time on our person, in case we wanted to buy something out of the machines or make calls, etc. So, I got on the city bus wearing jail clothes and went to my connections house, where I had started out in the first place. Once I arrived there, they told me that the police had been there looking for me and I needed to turn myself in. I told the dealer, that he owed me as I would not have gone to jail in the first place, had it not been for his wife. I told him that I wanted some cash, some clothes to change into, and some dope. They gave it to get rid of me, and I walked across the street and down to the off-ramp to the freeway and started hitching a ride to get out of California.

I finally made it to Mexico, where I got a job and a place to stay. It was easy for me since I taught myself to speak Spanish at a young age. You see, I wanted to be able to communicate with the Hispanic people, so I taught myself how to understand Spanish by listening and asking questions. Once I learned how to speak it, it was easy to teach myself how to read and write in Spanish as well! My only problem was that I still needed to find someone who could inject me with my dope without getting caught. I mean you can't just walk up to someone and say, "By the way, would you mind injecting me with my dope?!". It is kind of uncanny how one dope head can recognize another one from a mile away. As luck would have it, I met someone who was more than willing to help me out in exchange for some free dope. But I needed to find a syringe, as the one he wanted to use on me was used to give animals shots and it was HUGE; I was not going to let someone inject me with that huge thing. I would make trips back and forth from Mexico to the United States, just to buy syringes as I was too afraid to try to buy them in Mexico. I was in Juarez, Mexico so I did not have to go far to get what I needed once I crossed the border.

On one such trip, the immigration officer at the border said that I matched the description of a person who was wanted by the state of California. I told them that they were wrong, and the whole time we spoke, I refused to speak in English. All the way back to California I denied that I was the person that they were looking for, even after I had my fingerprints taken. They said that they could identify me, by the scars that I had on my knees and hands and by the fingerprints, and there was no doubt in their minds that I was who they were looking for.

Once I got to California, I was charged with escape from county jail. And I was taken to court and was given a year and a day in prison, as in the state of California at that time, anything under a year was county time and anything over a year was state time. So, they gave me a year and a day to send me to prison. I was sent to CIW (California Institution for Women) in Frontera, California first, then I was sent to a prison in Stockton, California. I did a little under a year there, and while I was there, I worked in electronics where we tore things apart and used the frames to make utility carts with. Doing California time is a picnic compared to doing Texas time. In California, inmates are allowed to have food packages and clothes sent in from home. The only thing we could not wear were khaki pants, as that was what the officers wore. When I was released from prison, they gave me $300 cash and instructed me to report to the parole office within 24 hours of my release from prison. I guess I did not learn my lesson very well, as once I got back "home" to Modesto, I went straight to the dope house and got some dope and rented a motel room for a couple of days. Once the dope and the money were gone, I hit the road again and went back to Mexico. First, I started in Mexico City and I found a job as a cocktail waitress, then soon thereafter as an apartment manager for the same boss. I worked there for a while until I got bored and had saved some money, and I decided to go to Cuernavaca, Mexico and got a job in a pizza/bar where I remained for 3 years.

After those three years, I got bored and decided to move on to Chihuahua, Mexico - a place called Durango. I had decided to go there, because when I was working and living in Mexico City, I met a guy named Jorge Alejandro Luna Rios (but he went by Jorge which is George in English) and I really liked him a lot. So, I thought I would just go there and look him up and take it from there. I finally found him and after spending a month there, with him paying for my motel room, I found out that I was pregnant. George would come to see me every night for the whole month that I was there. He would tell me that he was caring for his elderly mother, whom he lived with, and that is why he had to go home every night. I thought he was going to be happy when I told him that I was pregnant, but boy was I ever wrong! As soon as I told him that I was pregnant, he was quick to inform me that he was married. Yes, married, and that is why he really was never able to spend the night with me. So, here I was pregnant, all alone, as he was the only one that I knew there and now I was broke too. I did not have anyone to call for help and essentially, I was stuck.

The guys who ran the office at the motel where I had been staying for so long, were truly sympathetic to my plight but they had a job to do also, and since I did not have the money to pay for my room, they had to boot me out. They allowed me to stay one more night, and that night they did a raffle in the lobby, to get me some money to get back to the United States. I gave everyone I caught a ride with the same sad-but-true story about my situation, so they could understand why I was hitching a ride from Mexico to... yep, you guessed it... Medford, Oregon! Some of the truck drivers did not care that I was pregnant, they still wanted to have sex with me for a ride. Not all of them were that way; some of them were even kind enough to hook me up with rides with guys they knew, to be sure that I would be safe. And some of them not only fed me, but they gave me a few dollars to help me out as well. When I made it to California, a truck driver actually paid for a bus ticket, for me to make it the rest of the way home and gave me some money for food as well.

I found my mother and ended up moving in with her. My mom allowed me to stay there and had me sign up for food stamps and an AFDC check. I stayed with her for a long time. Eventually me, my mother, the daughter I gave birth to, and my little sister moved to Washington. We were going to stay with my oldest sister until we could find a place of our own.

At that time my sister and her husband had 2 little boys and lived in a trailer. After a couple of weeks, my mom and my sister started telling me that not only was I a terrible person, but a terrible mother as well. I had met a lady on the bus, when I was going back to Oregon from Mexico, who lived in Texas and she and I hit it off so well, that we exchanged phone numbers.

So, I called her and told her that I had to get away from my sister and my mother and why, and I asked her if I could go stay with her in Texas with my daughter until I could get on my feet. She spoke with her husband about it, then called me back and said that it would be okay for my baby and I to stay with her. So, as soon as I got my AFDC check and my food stamps, my baby, Mary, and I traveled to Texas to stay with my friend and get away from my mother and my sister.

It was not even a week after my arrival to Texas, when I was approached by my friend about the possibility of my giving my baby to her and her husband to raise. She tried to convince me that her and her husband could offer my daughter a better life than I ever could. She said that they could give me some money to get a fresh start somewhere else if I would allow them to adopt my daughter. My daughter looked more Mexican than she did white, and I began to fear that they might try to snatch my daughter and take her to Mexico, and I would never see her again. That weekend, they went to Mexico to see some family and again asked me to consider allowing them to adopt my daughter. After they left for Mexico, I called my mother and I begged her to please allow me to go back to them, as I feared that my friend and her husband were planning on stealing my baby and taking her to Mexico. I told her that I had nowhere else to go. She said no, but I did not believe that she would turn me and her grandbaby away.

So, I stole whatever I could find that could be sold, and I called a taxi and I had the driver take me to a pawn shop where I could sell the stuff and get the money, to buy a plane ticket back to Oregon. I arrived in Oregon and went to my mother's house. Yes, I said Oregon, my mother decided that she did not like it in Washington, so she decided to move back to Oregon. I don't think that Oregon ever stopped being home to my mother. Lucky for her, she had not been gone long enough for the landlady to rent out her apartment, so she was able to move back into the same place and was not required to pay a deposit. After about a month, the police showed up at my mom's house and told me that they had a warrant for my arrest for Burglary of a Habitat in the state of Texas. So, they told me to hand my baby over to my mother and put my hands behind my back.

My baby was only 9 months old and I cried uncontrollably, as the police car pulled away from my mother's house and my baby. I did not know how long it would be before I would get to see my baby again. I felt angry, as I felt completely justified in stealing from my friend, as I was sure that she was going to steal my baby, but no one wanted to hear about what she TRIED to do; they only cared about what I did do. I was extradited to the state of Texas, and I was charged and sentenced to 10 years and was sent to the Texas Department of Corrections. I thought that I was going to have to do the whole ten years and I did not know what I was going to do about my baby. I only ended up doing 10 months, but my mother made it seem like 10 years. While I was in TDCJ, my mother moved once again to the state of California, this time to be close to her sister. While I was in prison, my mother would keep me on an emotional roller coaster ride saying that she could not take care of my daughter and my little sister at the same time anymore, and if I did not find someone to come and get her, that she was going to give my daughter to CPS.

I finally got a cousin of mine to agree to take care of her until I got out, but then my mother said she would not give my daughter up. I know that the only reason why my mother was willing to take care of my daughter was because she was given a welfare check for keeping her and more food stamps as well. When I got out of prison, I had to have my parole transferred to California, where I would again move in with my mom and my little sister. My mom had gotten an apartment by the beach in a place called Daly City, California. My reunion with my daughter Mary was bittersweet, as she no longer knew me and whenever I would try to hold her, she would scream and cry and it broke my heart. I once again went on welfare and started my AFDC check again and my food stamps again, and again I gave most of it to my mother for the bills.

After a couple of months, I met a man who lived on the same floor as we did in the apartment building and I started dating him, and before I knew it - I was pregnant again! When I found out that I was pregnant, my mother told me that I needed to tell the guy I was dating, that I was pregnant. I asked her why, all he is going to do is say that it is not his. My mother said that if I did not tell him, that she would as she felt that he had a right to know. Because I had already been through the wringer with men like my daughter's father, I did not expect anything different from this guy. I really thought that he and I were doing well in our relationship, so I allowed myself to hope that he would be different than Jorge. So, I called Robert, and I told him that I needed to see him that night and he said okay. I thought he would be happy, as everything seemed to be going so good between us, and he even spent Christmas with me and my family. He had a great paying job working with the airlines, and he seemed to really like my daughter, so it all seemed good between us. But how wrong I was... once I told him that I was pregnant, the first thing that he said was, "It's not mine,".

I stared at him in shock and disbelief and hurt on my face. It was hard for me to believe that he was saying that the baby was not his, as I spent all of my spare time with him, and my mother would barely take care of my daughter for me to be able to have any alone time with him. Nonetheless, to spend any time with anyone else, so I could not believe that he could even question that it was his baby. I was hurt, angry, and bitter as I loved Robert and I would never have expected him to react that way. I ran out of Robert's apartment and went to the floor below ours, where I had a friend who was also a single parent of a little girl. She had a beautiful little girl who was around my daughter's age, and she would give me the clothes and the shoes that her daughter could no longer use. Upon returning to the apartment that I shared with my mom, she asked me what Robert said when I told him that I was pregnant. I told her that he said it was not his, and I ran out of his apartment full of hurt, anger, and pain. She asked me what I was going to do, now that we knew that Robert was not going to take responsibility for the baby that I was carrying? I told her that I guess I was going to become a single parent again!

The next day, I went to see my friend again and visited with her and her mother who was helping her raise her daughter's baby. When I got back to my apartment, my mom said that Robert had been by and had dropped off some groceries, and I took them back to him and told him that I did not need his pity, nor did I want his help. I told him if it was not his baby then my needs did not concern him. I went down to the manager's office and spoke with the manager, as she and I had become friends after I had moved in with my mom. When I told her what had happened with Robert, she gave me a hug and told me it would be okay! The very next day, my mother told me that I had to move out. I asked her why, and she said that it was because I was not on her HUD certificate, and she would get into trouble if they found out that I was living there with her. and she could not afford to have her and her daughter kicked out.   But my friend the manager told me, that it was my mother who wanted me to leave and that HUD had nothing to do with it. I was angry and hurt and lost and did not have a clue of what I was going to do next.

I called my aunt and I told her what was happening, and she and my uncle went to Catholic Charities in Daly City and got them to give me the money that I would need to move into a place of my own. I found a place in Daly City, that I could afford to rent from an Oriental couple who had a bunch of rooms in their house and in their garage that they rented out. I got a room in their garage for $250 plus my power. My aunt and uncle helped me get a microwave and a coffee pot and a bed as well as a mini fridge, and that is all my daughter and I had besides our clothes. We shared a bathroom with several other people. My next problem was that I had to find a job and someone who could look after my daughter while I went to work. I only needed a job until I could get my AFDC check and food stamps started again. I was still on parole for the state of Texas, so I had to report the change of address to the parole officer, so that I would not get into trouble for failure to report my new address. Robert found out where I moved to (through my mom, who found out through my aunt I'm sure), and he showed up there wanting to take me to my doctor appointments and wanted to bring me some groceries and I told him NO, that I did not want or need his help. I told him, that he said that it was not his baby that I was carrying, so it was not his responsibility to make sure I get to the doctor or have food or anything else. I told him that it was not any of his business.

I got a job working as a barmaid in a bar not far from where I lived, and my landlady told me about a Mexican lady who took care of kids, so I got ahold of the lady and she agreed to take care of my daughter. I worked at the bar until I started showing and the boss said that he could not have a pregnant woman working in his bar. Thank God it happened at the same time that I got my welfare check started. I had been allowing my daughter to talk to my mother on the phone, as she loved her Nana, and I did not have the heart to keep her from her Nana because my mom and I had problems. I think that my aunt and uncle gave her grief for having thrown my daughter and I out, so she had once again decided to move back to Oregon. I told my mother that she may as well just stay there as she always went back.

My mother was the queen of manipulation, a skill that she taught my little sister well! Since I knew this, and I did not trust my mom, I would put the phone on speaker phone so I could hear what my mother would say to my daughter. I heard her tell my daughter that she loved and missed her, and my mother would cry and make my daughter cry too. I finally had to tell my mother that I would no longer allow her to speak to my daughter if she was going to continue to upset her. My mom told me, if I would just stop being stubborn and move to Oregon, that she and my daughter would not have to miss each other and continue to be upset. She said that she would even come and get us and help me to move. So, with much dread and a heavy heart, I agreed to move back to Oregon, and I thought with my mother. Once she got to California and packed us up to go back to Oregon, my mom asked me if I realized that I had to pay for the gas to get us back to Oregon and I also owed her for the gas that it took her to get there. I could not believe what she was saying. She had never said anything about me having to pay her for helping me move back to Oregon; she was the one that wanted me to move there with her!

Upon arriving in Medford, I made yet another horrifying discovery, my mother was living with an old friend of mine who had turned her back on me because of my mother's lies, and she did not want me in her house!

I had to use the bathroom, but my mother would not allow me to go into the house to use the bathroom, even though the lady was at that moment in Mexico as my mother feared that a neighbor would see me going into the house and tell mom's friend. I could not wait any longer to use the bathroom, so I had to squat behind a bush by the house like a dog to go pee. Then another realization hit me, if my mother was living with her friend and I was not allowed in her house, then where were Mary and I going to live? I had already given my mother all the money I had for food and gas, and I would not get a check for a while, as I would have to go to the welfare office and have my checks restarted... and not only that, but I still had to report to parole.

I made some calls and I found out where my mother's ex-boyfriend Buster lived, and I went to his trailer house, and I told him what had happened with my eyes filled with tears and a heavy heart. Buster allowed me and my daughter to stay there, until one day my mother and little sister arrived there and asked if they could stay there as well, as her friend had kicked them out of her house and she and my little sister did not have anywhere else to go. He told her no, that they could not stay there, as his trailer was too small for so many people and that he would get into trouble for having so many people staying there. So, my mother and my little sister stayed in her car and left it parked outside of his trailer, and after a few days the security of the trailer park told Buster that my mom could not stay in her car there and she had to go. He was kind enough to give us a few days to find somewhere else to go. I am sure that that was my mother's plan all along; remember I said that she was the queen of manipulation!

So, my mother and I started looking for place to move to, but neither one of us could afford a place on our own. So, once again we looked for a place that we could share. We found a nice newly built apartment and it was in a good location. But the Hud certificate was only for 2 bedrooms, so my mom and my little sister would have to share a room, and my daughter and I would have to share a room. I could not afford a bed, so I had to sleep on a mattress on the floor with my daughter. As you can imagine, it was hard for me to get up and down from the floor with my being 6 months pregnant. I had a huge stomach and small arms and legs. Once my son was born, my mother decided that it was time for me to go as she no longer needed me, my money, or my food stamps... or perhaps she simply decided that she no longer wished to share the home? Either way, I was back to square one once again! Here I was a single parent with a two-year-old daughter, a two-day-old baby and I had once again already paid my mother my share of everything - I had given her all my food stamps for the month, so I was broke, with nowhere to go and two kids. I took my daughter and my newborn son, and I put them in a double stroller I had and went walking and crying all the way to my grandma's house, and I told her what had happened. I told her that I did not know what I was going to do. My grandma talked to her landlady, and she agreed to allow me and my kids to stay with her until I could find a place of my own.

It was my 24th birthday, and my mother had the nerve to call my grandma's house and say that she wanted to go to my grandma's house and help me to celebrate my birthday and to visit her grandchildren. My grandma and my mom had words, and my mom made my grandma cry. I had gone to the welfare office to try to get emergency funds, so I could get a place to live, then I went looking for a place and the call from my mother had come while I was gone. I got to my grandma's and saw her crying, and I asked her why she was crying, and she told me what happened. I finally got my grandma to calm down, and I called my mother and gave her a piece of my mind. I told her that she could not have it both ways, to kick me and my kids out and still want to have a part of our lives. My mother was spiteful, resentful, and full of revenge. She did not like me putting her in her place and she decided to get even with me.

In the meantime, my grandmother's landlady told her that my children and I would have to leave, as it was a home for seniors and that there simply was not enough room for the four of us. At the same time, I got a phone call from Robert's mom (my son's father's mother_ at 3:00 in the morning, as my mother had given her my number. She wanted to know when I was going to allow her son to see his baby? I told her that first of all, Robert had claimed from the beginning that he was not the baby's father and second of all, as far as I knew she was dead as he never even mentioned his mother to me. Robert had never discussed his family, so I had no idea how this woman had suddenly become a part of my life! Of course, there was only one way that she and her son could have found me and that is through my mother! I told her that if Robert was so concerned about "his son ", then when was he going to start helping me to care for his son? I told her that her grandson, my two-year-old daughter and I were about to become homeless, and he is not even trying to help me. She had the nerve to tell me, that once I had a paternity test done to prove that Robert was the baby's father, that she was sure that he would take responsibility for the baby. I told her that I did not have any money to feed our son, nonetheless to pay for a paternity test! So, she had Robert send me some money via Western Union. I went to pick up the money and was sooo mad and embarrassed, when not only did I see that all he sent me was $75 but he also added a note saying, "No more money till DNA results "! I was embarrassed, because I knew that other people had read that note, and I could only imagine what thoughts must have been going through their minds as they read or wrote those words. Later, I found out that my mother had told him to send me the money Western Union, so he could prove that he had sent it and I had received the money, so that he could report it to welfare as unreported child support, as I had to report any money that I received to welfare and I could be charged with welfare fraud and could face charges and lose my welfare checks...

My grandma paid for me to get a haircut, so I would feel better about myself, then she took me to an apartment that she had found for my kids and I. She had taken the money out of her savings account to help me get into the apartment and it was all bills paid. It was a little studio apartment, but it was perfect for my children and I. After about a month of living in this apartment, my mother began to insinuate herself into our lives again. She and my little sister would come by and want us to go on a walk with them, and like an idiot, I once again allowed my mother back into my life.

One day as we were on one of our walks, I had to stop walking long enough to switch arms, as I was pushing a stroller with one hand and I was carrying my son in my arm and my arm began to fall asleep. As I attempted to switch him over to my other arm, somehow the blanket that he was wrapped in got caught up and I ended up dropping him on the concrete sidewalk. I started screaming and panicked and did not know what to do. I did not have a car or money for the bus, so I called a friend to give us a ride to the emergency room. My friend said that she did not have enough room in her small truck for the four of us to ride and the baby would have to be put in the car seat. So, I asked her to please take my baby to the emergency room and I would give her a letter giving her permission, to get medical help for my son until I could arrive, and if the hospital had any questions before I got there that they could call me. She handed me a paper that was one of her kid's school papers and it had one side blank, and I wrote a quick note giving the hospital permission to treat my son, and I added my phone number so I could be reached if necessary before I could get to the hospital. So, she agreed to take him to the hospital and tell them that I would soon be there. I called my grandma crying frantically and I told her what happened, and I told her that Mary and I needed a ride to the hospital. My grandmother came to pick us up and took us to the hospital, and by the grace of God, the doctor said that my son was going to be okay! My mother decided to use this as an opportunity to cause me trouble. She called Robert and told him that I had been high on drugs and that I had dropped our son onto the concrete, and that thank God he was going to be okay, but who knows for how long if he was left in my care! Then she called the parole office and told my parole officer that I was high on drugs, and that I had dropped my son on the concrete as a result of being high! But she was not done there, she then called CPS and told them the same story and gave them Roberts name and number, so that he could be contacted.

After that, I refused to allow her to come around ever again and I would not allow her to see or talk to her grandchildren. I was tired of her crap and I was tired of her trying to cause me trouble and pain. I had finally had enough! I could not believe what my own mother was trying to do, to destroy me and my life. Then she started sending people over to spy on me and to see how my kids were and if my house was clean. Suddenly, people who I had not seen in years began to drop by, and family members who had not come to see me in months began to drop by - and they were all sent by my mother.

She was trying to get parole to revoke me, so that she could have my daughter and get the money that welfare would give her for taking care of my daughter, and my son would go to his father. Of course, when my son had his accident, because of her accusations, they tested me for drugs as did the parole office, but they found nothing so there was nothing that they could do to me. But that did not stop my mother; she was determined to take everything from me, and she would tell anyone who would listen that I was doing drugs again! I began getting paranoid and could not sleep, and I became obsessive in cleaning my house and in keeping my children clean at all times. Before I knew it, there was a knock on my door and CPS had sent a worker to my house to check on me, my children, and my house. Then I got a court order to appear in court to fight for custody of my son. My son's father had decided that it was time for him to take me to court to fight for my son. My son was only a couple of months old at the time and I was scared to death that I was going to lose him. All of my past insecurities started coming back to me, and I began to have thoughts of what a bad person and mother I was, that I did not deserve my children and a life with them, and all kinds of doubts came creeping back into my mind. All of my father's past words came flooding back into my mind, that I was worthless and that I would never amount to anything, and I would never truly be loved or wanted by anyone. I had so much against me and so little going for me, or at least in my mind! I had a felonious background. I was an addict and a single mother on welfare, and Robert had a great job, no record, and he had paid my mother to go against me in court! What chance did I have of winning?

I lost before court ever began... When he arrived in Oregon from California, he brought his mother with him, so that she could help him with my son in the event that he won custody. Robert did win custody of my son because first, I did not even bother going to court. You see, I had already decided that there was no way I could possibly win. After all, as my father said, I would never be anything and I was a terrible person, and why would so many people be against me if I was a good person?! So, I decided to stay in my apartment with my children and say goodbye to my son, which at the time I decided was a better way to spend the time.

The social worker had a court order to take my son to his father and told me that I had an hour to gather my son's things together, so his father could come pick them up. I was forced to let go of my son, as he was torn from my arms, and my daughter and I cried loudly as my son was taken away from us. When Robert arrived to take my son's things from me, he did not bring my son, so I could say goodbye to him as he felt it was not in my son's best interest! When my son was born, I named him after my grandfather Harvey Glenn Hulse, as I had always heard such great things about my grandfather. I never met him because he died when my mother was a young girl. So, I thought it would be cool to honor him by naming him after my grandfather. When Robert got custody of my son, the first thing that he did was change my son's name to Robert Newborn Ford after himself. My troubles and my heartache still were not over, as CPS was still in my life with my daughter. By the way, I had named my daughter Mary after my mother, as many years before I had promised her that I would name my first-born daughter after her.

I was being made to take UA's by both CPS and parole, and I finally had come to the conclusion that my mother would not be happy until I lost EVERYTHING that was important to me. So, I called an aunt of mine and I asked her to come and get my daughter, as I knew that my mother was not going to be happy until I lost everything that mattered to me and I couldn't take it anymore. My aunt said that the only way that she would take my daughter, is if I would allow her and my uncle to adopt her, because they did not want to invest their time, money, and love into her and then I would come back and want to take her back. So, I agreed to her terms, and she came to Oregon and I gave my daughter to them.

Now I would have CPS out of my life, and my mother off my back, and I would no longer have my children who were ALL I cared about in the world and they were the only thing that kept me clean. Since I no longer had anything to live for, I gave up on life that day. I did not care if I was free anymore, and I did not care about staying clean anymore, and I started hanging out in bars and sleeping around and doing drugs. I no longer had a place to live as I could not bear living in a place where I once lived with my children. I partied a lot and stayed high all of the time. I figured, that as long as I stayed high, I would not have to feel the pain of losing my children and I would not be in any condition to think at all, nonetheless about my kids who I loved and lost. I violated my parole by giving up on reporting and getting high and not having an address to give them for my residence. It was inevitable that sooner or later I would get picked up for being under the influence, and when I did, I would get sent back to Texas for violation of parole. I was picked up under the influence of Methamphetamines, and they ran my name through the database, and they found a warrant for me for violation of parole and they held me for the state of Texas to come get me. Once I was released from TDCJ, I was sent to a halfway house in Fort Worth, Texas. I had to stay there until I could get a job and save the money to get my own place since I did not have anyone here.

Now, I am going to skip forward a little to where I got a job at a place called Sonterra Apartments, where I was trained to be a Leasing Agent, and I was given an apartment on property. I was 34 years old and single, and I met a guy that lived in the apartments where I worked, and he and I became lovers. We were lovers for quite some time, and for the first time in a long time, I felt loved and needed and wanted and felt like I was living in some kind of fantasy world. It seems to me that whenever things seem to be going better than ever, that inevitably something happens to destroy my happiness. So, whenever I got close to being happy, I would find a way to make it self-destruct because I knew that true happiness was not something that I would ever have! I mean, I had a good job, an apartment, a man who seemed to adore me as much as I adored him, and my aunt and uncle had traveled from California to bring my now half-grown daughter to see me. How much better could things get than that? Not long after my daughter and aunt and uncle left, I found out that I was once again pregnant. And again, once I found out that I was pregnant and I told my boyfriend that I was pregnant, he told me that he was married! And there it was - my world came tumbling down around me. I was so angry and hurt that I found out, that in fact the "friend" he was sharing an apartment with was actually his wife... I went to the apartment and knocked on the door, and I introduced myself to his wife, and I told her that I was pregnant by her husband. I told her that I was sorry and had not known that he was married, or I would never had been with him. She said that she was sorry for my dilemma, and this was not the first time that this had happened, that it was the 8th pregnancy outside of their marriage. I could not believe what I was hearing. I asked her why she would stay with a lying, cheating man like that? She said it was because she loved him. It did not take long for me to realize, that she was very codependent on him, and she had a little boy with him. Once my boss found out that I was pregnant by a married resident of the apartments, I was fired, and I lost my apartment in the same day. So, here I was pregnant and single with a baby on the way again, and I did not know what I was going to do.

My boyfriend's wife and I became fast friends and she insisted on helping me through this. She introduced me to a Christian couple who went to her church and babysat for her son. Barbara and Ray were their names, and she had told them what had happened, and she asked them to allow me to live with them till the baby was born, and I could get a job and get on my feet. They were a very kind and loving Christian couple, and they agreed to help me out. They took me to church with them, and they introduced me to the pastor and his wife, and they made sure I made all of my doctor appointments and took me to get on food stamps so I would have plenty of nutrition. Barbara and Ray treated me like I was one of the family. It hurt me to see my ex, every time that he came to drop his son off at the house, as it brought up painful memories. Barbara did not judge me, and she was loving and patient with me, and she and I talked about what my future plans were, and she was there with me when I gave birth to my daughter. I asked Barbara and Ray if I could honor and thank them by naming my daughter after them. Barbara said that she never liked her name and she asked me to name her Victoria. Since Ray is a man's name, I named her Victoria Rae using a different spelling for a girl. My daughter was a beautiful little girl and I loved her so much from the very first time that I laid eyes on her.

I waited a couple of weeks and then I went looking for a job, and I ended up getting a job as a van driver, and Barbara and Ray would take care of my baby while I was at work. Things still were not great because it had been a long time since I had reported to parole, and I knew that there was probably a warrant out for my arrest, and I did not want to lose my baby! I could not bear the thought of going through that again. I went and spoke to the pastor of our church and come to find out, he was into prison ministry and he knew people through parole. So, he agreed to speak to parole on my behalf, and they agreed to reinstate my parole and not violate me on a probationary basis. I was still going to church after I got a job and it was there, that I met a very nice, sweet lady who I became good friends with, and she eventually introduced me to her brother. After a few months we ended up living together, and Barbara and Ray did not like him and did not think that he was good for Rae and me. They said that if I wanted to continue to see him that Rae and I would have to move out. So, my friend's brother and I ended up moving in together. I thought that I was finally going to be happy. But that was not to be. He was an alcoholic and while I was working two different shifts at Walmart, he stayed home to take care of my baby and his definition of taking care of her was leaving her in a play pen and drinking with one of his other sisters. He finally got a job out of town and made a deal with me, that I would stay home and take care of Rae Rae (this is what everyone called my daughter at the time.) while he worked in Hondo, and I would go to Hondo once a month to spend the weekend with him and he would come home once a month to see us.

One weekend that he came home he decided to buy a car from his niece, and I was supposed to go get insurance on the car. It was raining that day, so I was going to leave my daughter with his sister who lived close by and who babysat for us from time to time. On the way to his sister's house, I was driving 35 miles an hour and went around the corner, and my car slid, and lost traction and I lost control of the car. The car slid and spun around, and I hit a huge brick and concrete mailbox, and then the car jumped a ditch and hit the phone pole that was there. Amazingly, the car was still running until I shut it off. There was a man across the field across the street who had heard the crash and had called for help. My daughter was in the back seat in her car seat (thank God) and I was in the front seat, and I think I was still in shock. The roof of the car was caved in, the back window was shattered as was the front window, and the right side of the car was smashed in. By the grace of God, neither one of us were hurt. As a matter of fact, neither one of us had a scratch on us! Now that is a miracle in itself! There were a couple of EMT's that lived around the corner and were the first to arrive at the scene of the accident. They asked me if I believed in God? I said, "Yes, I do, why?" They said that by the looks of the car, my daughter and I both should have been either killed or badly injured, and we were neither. The car however, was a different story. Since I had not been able to get the insurance before I had the accident, and the car was totally wrecked, there was nothing that I could do about the car. When the police arrived, they asked if there was someone, they could call to come pick my daughter and I up, since the EMT's had cleared us and suggested that someone take us to the hospital for a more thorough checkup. So, I had them call my sister in law and she came, and she called my husband and told him what had happened, and then she handed me the phone. He started screaming and said that he did not know what we were going to do, since we did not have insurance on the car. I was shocked, he did not even ask if the baby and I were okay, and that hurt me so much. But I loved him, so I let it go.

One time when he came home from Hondo, he got very sick and had to go to the hospital. I was so worried about him, that the baby and I stayed at the hospital with him, until we were sure that he was okay. I was scared, and I thought that he was going to die and leave me and the baby alone. After the first night, the doctor approached me and said that the baby and I needed to be tested! I was shocked, what could they possibly want to test the baby and I for? He said that my husband had Hepatitis C and that he had had it for a very long time, and there was a chance that he had given it to her and I! I told them that there was no reason to test the baby, as she was not his biological child, so they tested me for Hep. C and I came out positive! I could not believe what I was hearing. Not only did he have hepatitis C, but he had sex with me, knowing that he could infect me and did not care.

I had been blessed in not getting Hepatitis or any other disease through the years of IV use and now I get hepatitis through making love to a man who I loved. I felt betrayed, hurt, angry and worthless.

He finally got better, and he went back to work, and one day he got a call from one of his nephews who did not like me saying that I was trying to buy drugs from him. My husband broke speeding records trying to get back home from Hondo and started yelling accusations at me, and he would not believe anything that I would say. He told me that he was taking my daughter away from me and that I would never see her again! I could not find my daughter anywhere and I was going crazy. I called the police, and they said that they could not do anything about it, as my husband supported us and the fact that we were married, it gave him as much rights as I had to her and that it was a civil matter.

So, I stole some of our checks from our joint bank account and started getting drunk, and I met someone (a next-door neighbor) that sold drugs and I bought some drugs from them and asked them to help inject me. The drunker I got, the more drugs I did, and the hotter checks I wrote. You see, the only way that I knew how to deal with trouble was to run to drugs. It was the only way that I knew "out of trouble". It was no time at all, before I was going to jail for theft by check and I had to serve four years in prison. My husband would bring my daughter to see me and he would put money on my books, and everything seemed okay. Then he started telling me that he and his ex-sister-in-law, were scamming a guy she knew out of money from his credit card, and that he was putting money on my books from this guy's money. He talked a lot about this ex-sister-in-law, and I started getting suspicious about their relationship.

Before it was time for my release, he told me that he was hooking up with her, and I had been writing to a friend of mine in a men's prison who was a paralegal. He said he could draw up some papers for a friend of his to get temporary guardianship until I got out, and I could be released to her, as she had a Christian halfway house. So, I told him to do it. Once she got the paperwork finalized, I told her where my daughter's aunt lived - where I was sure my daughter was and I told her to take the police with her, to execute the order to hand over my daughter and not to go alone.

Instead, Rosie tried to go get her alone and scared my daughter when she tried to snatch her, and my sisters-in law were there, and they jumped on Rosie and took my daughter and put her in a car and ran off with her. So, my husband took my daughter and hid her, so when I got out, I could not find her. He filed with the court for full custody and when I arrived at the courthouse with Rosie, I saw him sitting there with his ex-sister-in-law (and now lover). We got into a big argument in the courthouse and the judge kicked us out and said not to come back until we had an attorney. My husband and his lover left the courthouse and took off before I could say anything else. I continued to search for my daughter, and I could never get the money for an attorney, so things were left as they were.

I went back to the only thing I knew - drugs. At the time, I did not know that it would be years before I would see my daughter again. Little did I know at the time, that my ex-husband had told my daughter that I had died of a drug overdose and that he had seen it on the news. Over time, he had convinced her that I had chosen drugs over her. She grew up hating me and missing having me around at the same time.

I got involved with a man who was 20 years older than me, and he was controlling, and he would always introduce me as "his white girl"; he was a Hispanic man. He got me a job at a store called Thrift Town and I moved in with him. I had to give him all of my money and I was not allowed to have any friends, but his friends, and I was told where I could go and when I could go. One of his friends that I was allowed to be friends with was a lady who bought Meth from him. Her name was Prieta and she was always very nice to me. She was the only one that Chuco allowed to cut his hair because he had to have his hair done a certain way. Prieta and I became fast friends and she did not like the way that he treated me. She and I did drugs together when Chuco was at work and her husband was also at work. She was a lonely soul and she was a good-hearted soul. She would also buy dope from Chuco's nephew, who also in time became my friend. Prieta and I did a lot of things together, and I always looked forward to seeing her, because she made me laugh. I thought that I was in love with him and I thought the the world revolved around him. He helped me make it through the rest of my parole and I finally got off of parole. His name was Chuco, and I treated him like a king. I cooked for him, cleaned for him, and took care of his dogs and from time to time, I took care of his grandchildren at no charge. I did not know that he was selling large amounts of marijuana and some meth on the side. He introduced me to his friends and some of his family. He had two rooms in his house that he rented out, one to an old friend of his. He would make me go with him to the cabaret and watch naked women dance, and he would dictate what I had to wear and what I wore had to match whatever he wore. My brother Perry came to visit from Oregon, while I was with Chuco and I got him a job working at the bindery where I was working at the time. I got him a job there, so he could make the money to catch the bus home when he got ready to go, because I did not want him to hitchhike back to Oregon.

I was so angry with Richard (a friend of Chuco's who rented from Chuco), because I asked them not to get my brother involved with drugs as he drank but he never did drugs. Richard and his friends got Perry high, and I was already asleep, and I did not know that they had given him some Meth. Perry started tripping saying that he saw someone get killed and was seeing things. He was hallucinating, while running wild and alone in the streets, and Richard was worried because Perry was only supposed to go to the store up the street to get some beer and had not returned... so he woke me up and told me what happened. I was both angry and worried, and I went out looking for him and thank God I found him.

When I got back to the house I started yelling at Richard and his friends, and I told them that it was not cool that they got my brother high, especially after I had specifically asked them not to. Their answer to my rant was that my brother was a grown man and if he wanted to try something then I did not have the right to stand in his way. It was not long after this that I put my brother on the bus back to Oregon. I did not want him to get tied up with drugs and that is what I feared would happen if he stayed here. One day, I came home from work and I wanted to drink a beer, but Chuco said I was not allowed to drink anymore. I asked what was going on and he said it did not matter why, all that mattered is that he said that I could not drink anymore. I was sooo mad, I told his friend Richard what Chuco said, and Richard told me that Chuco had received a call from (of all people) my mother who I had not seen in years! Apparently, Perry had been talked into giving my mother my phone number, and she called, and she told Chuco not to let me drink, as I was an alcoholic! Boy was I mad; my mother had interfered for the last time! I got her number off of his phone and I called her, and I told her that if she was going to tell someone something about me at least get it right - I am not the alcoholic, that is my brother - I am the addict! I told her that she had gone too far this time and that as far as I am concerned, she was dead! I told her not to call me and that I would not call her, ever. It was around then that Chuco started to be abusive towards me and he would put me down and talk trash to me and was mean.

One day his nephew came to the house and he had a white guy with him, and the white guy asked him, "Who is that lady?" He was talking about me, and Chuco's nephew told him that I was his uncle's old lady. One day, Chuco came home and said that I would have to stay in the guest room because he was bringing another lady home. I told him that I loved him, and I thought that he felt the same way. He said that he had never told me that he loved me, and if I did not like him bringing someone else home, then I knew what I could do. He told me this in front of his nephew, and his nephew's friend whose name was Larry. Richard was also there. Chuco knew that I had nowhere else to go so I had no choice but to put up with the way that he treated me. I tried to overdose on pills that night. I took a bunch of them and I passed out on the kitchen floor, and I was coming around when I heard Richard asking Chuco what they were going to do if I died, and Chuco said that they would dump my body off somewhere as he was not going to allow my stupidity to get him sent to prison! I went to Prieta's house the next day and I told her what had happened, and I told her that my heart was broken. She called Chuco's nephew and told him that she wanted some meth and asked if he could bring her some.

He got to her house and saw me there and was surprised to see me there. I told him what had happened the night before with his uncle and I told him that my heart was broke. He asked me why I put up with it, and I said because I had no family here in Texas, and I had nowhere to go. I asked him if I could go and stay with him and his wife for a little while, until I could figure out what to do. I ended up staying at the nephew's house awhile, and then I realized that he and his wife had problems and they fought all of the time. One day, about 2 weeks after I had been staying at Chuco's nephews house, I decided that I could not take all of the fighting anymore and I would be better off back at Chuco's.

Chapter Five: Larry

My Husband

My husband always says that he will be the first one to go
I love him with all my heart, maybe even more than he will ever know
He has stood by my side through so much from the start

And now that we have been together for 12 years, I cant't imagine us ever being apart
My baby's health is so bad that I always fear that his prediction may come true
Whenever I think of him dying I get real sad and my heart breaks in two
He is a great provider, and a loving husband and a great son too
If he does die first, I will be so lost Lord, without him what will I do
Sometimes when I cant't sleep I look at him sleeping with a peaceful look on his face
If he is worried about anything there are no signs, not a single trace
He has such a big heart and will do what ever needs to be done
Oh Lord, what am I going to do if I lose the man who I have loved for these last few years
Just the thought of it breaks my heart and fills me with so many fears
Oh Lord, please don't let my husband die first and leave me here all alone,
don't let us die apart
I don't want to live without him, I don't want to carry that pain in my heart...

That day, Larry showed up at Chuco's nephew's house and I asked him if he thought that Larry would give me a ride back to Northside. He asked Larry, and Larry said that if I didn't mind riding on a motorcycle, then he would be happy to give me a ride. He asked me if I would allow him to take me to Dairy Queen to get something to eat and I said sure. So, we went to the Dairy Queen on Northside and we ate, and we talked, and he asked me why I put up with Chuco. I told him that I had no one here and that I had nowhere else to go. When we were finished, he gave me his phone number and said that if I ever needed anything to let him know, then he asked me where he was going to drop me off and I told him that I wanted him to drop me off at Prieta's house, as she just lived around the corner from Chuco. And I did not want Chuco to see him dropping me off. He asked if he could take me with him to his house to drop off his bike and pick up his truck as it looked like it was going to rain. I said sure. So, we went to his house to pick up his truck and then we went to Prieta's house, and no sooner than we arrived Chuco pulled up behind us. Oh boy, I knew that I was in for it now. He came to the truck and asked me why I looked like a slut? Give me a break, I was wearing a pair of jeans and a t-shirt! I asked him why he said I looked like a slut and he said because he said so. He told me to get out of the truck and into his car, and he told

Larry that I gave him a yeast infection, so he hoped that I had not had sex with him! That night, Chuco and I got into a big fight and I told him to go to hell, and I walked out. It was pouring rain and I didn't even know what I was going to do or where I was going to go and I really didn't care, I just wanted to get away from the jerk and I figured that it would be better than putting up with Chuco. Then I remembered the phone number in my pocket that Larry had given me, and I decided to call him. He seemed nice enough and he seemed to care about my situation so why not call him. Besides, it was pouring rain outside, and I was both wet and cold. So, I called Larry and I told him what happened, and I told him that I did not know what I was going to do. So, he said he would go pick me up but that I would have to meet him somewhere else, as he did not want Chuco to know that he was helping me. So, he came and picked me up, and we snuck into his room as he lived with his parents in their house. He held me in his arms as I cried and talked about how much I loved Chuco and how unfair it was that he treated me the way he did. Larry did not try to push himself on me, he only held me and listened to what I had to say. He said that he thought that I should give Chuco one more chance as it was obvious that I loved him. So, once again I returned to Chuco's and I begged him for another chance. Larry would come by and check on me while Chuco was at work, to see if I was okay and to get me high. One day, Chuco noticed that I had track marks on my arm, and he said I had to go because he was not going to have a junkie whore in his house or in his life. So, I told Larry the next day what Chuco said, and he told me that even if I did not want to be with him that he would help me to get into a place of my own and then I could pay him back as I was able.

So that night, I spent the night with him and every night after that. After only two months of being with Larry- drinking, having sex and doing drugs together, we decided to get married. I had sworn after my marriage to my ex-husband that marriage was not for me and that I would never get married again, yet here I was agreeing to marry Larry. I told Larry that before the justice of the peace marries us, he better make sure that it is what he wants. I told him because once the justice of peace says till death do us part, I mean till death do us part which means one of us will die before we could divorce. I told him, and then it would be a murder-suicide as I was not going to prison for killing him!

About a month after Larry and I were married, Larry and his parents got the money together for me to go to my first family reunion ever! It would be the first time in 10 years that I had seen my daughter Mary and I was really nervous about it, because I had been hating myself for so many years because I felt as though I had let my daughter down because I gave her to my aunt and uncle, and I was sure that she hated me. Not only that, but my mother was there, and I had not spoken to her since our phone conversation when I was with Chuco. Also, I had always promised myself when I was a child that if I ever had kids that I would always make sure that they knew that they were wanted, needed and loved, and I felt that I failed when it came time to do as I said I would do. Our family reunion is in August of every year on my Aunt's farm and they always have so much food and so many people. I had almost convinced myself that it would be better if I did not go, and I called Mary to tell her I was not sure about going, because her Nana and I had not spoken in years and I did not want to cause trouble. She begged me to go and she said that I would have her and my uncle there to protect me from my mother. So, we went but I told Larry that if we went, we needed to stay away from drugs while we were there because I did not want anyone to know that I was still active in my addiction and he agreed. When we arrived at my cousin's house, my daughter was not there. My cousin said that my daughter was not going to be there until the next day! I was sad and disappointed that my daughter would not be there until the next day. My cousin said that we could stay at her house until after the family reunion. Happily, my daughter did show up that night, as Larry and I were sitting on the front porch and when we saw each other, we both took off running towards one another and we both were crying, and we hugged each other and cried some more. I then asked my daughter with tears in my eyes and fear in my heart to forgive me for not being there for her while she was growing up. She said, "Mom, there is nothing to forgive". She said that I gave her life, and when I saw that I was not able to care for her, that I gave her to someone who I knew would not abuse her and would love her! She also told me that every year on her birthday she does not celebrate the years of her life, she celebrates me and the fact that I gave her life. I felt a great sense of relief that day, and I felt a heavy weight come off my shoulders, that I had been carrying for so long and had become so heavy... knowing that my daughter did not hate me and that she never had hated me! My mother was at the family reunion and I was shocked to see how fat she had gotten! I was telling Larry that I had never seen my mother so fat, and then I heard someone crying and turned around to see my mother running away crying, because she had overheard what I had said about her. I felt bad, but you can't undo something that you say after you have said it. Larry and I enjoyed the rest of the day at the family reunion and we really enjoyed all the wonderful food that they had there. After the family reunion, Larry and I decided to go to Medford, Oregon to see some more of my family who I had not seen in 20 years or more. It was not a long drive from Homedale, Idaho to Medford, or at least it did not seem like a long way. Larry was so shocked when we stopped at a gas station on the Oregon side of the border, as in the state of Oregon self-service gas stations do not exist. He could not believe that it was a law that you could not pump your own gas.

We wanted some dope so bad we could not stand it. We had no money to buy any, but I convinced Larry that I could convince my little brother to give us some of his stash. So, Larry and I headed to Medford and to see my brother and once we arrived, we started looking for him. It was not easy to find my little brother. We tried to find out through family how to find my brother, but no one would answer their phones. We went to a few places where I knew someone would know my brother and we did finally get ahold of someone who knew my little brother, and they called him and gave him my number. We finally got ahold of my aunt and she told us that we could stay at her house. As it was late, and we were not sure if my brother would ever call us back and we were tired, we agreed to stay at her house. About 2:00 in the morning my brother called, and he said if we wanted something to meet him at the WalMart in Medford. He was high and scared, as he was hiding from the feds, as they had him on drug charges. He had a police scanner in his car, and he told us to follow him. He made us follow him all over the place before he finally stopped at a gas station and got out and was pretending to put air in a tire, as he passed me a bag of dope and gave me a hug and disappeared. Larry and I went down an alley and did a shot and got so high that we saw a washer and dryer that was on a curb, and we loaded it up into the back of the truck and intended to take it to Texas to recycle, that is how high we were. After that, Larry and I got on the freeway and headed for home. When we were going down the freeway at 60 miles an hour, Larry pounded his fist on the dash of the truck while driving, and I asked him what was the matter? He said that rationally, he knew that what he was seeing in the mirror was not real, but it looked so real. I asked him what he was seeing, and he said that he saw a pelican on the dryer, and it was staring at him and making a strange sound. He said that the funny thing was, that the pelican was on the back of the dryer in the back of the truck going 60 miles an hour, and it did not have a single feather out of place! I told him "Damn baby, I think that maybe it is time for me to drive"!

So, I took over driving while Larry slept, and I have such a bad sense of direction that I thought that I would get lost. I found the way back to Texas, but as soon as I got to Texas, I pulled up at the mint in Saginaw in the middle of the night and there were men there with guns and bright lights! I woke Larry up, and I told him that we were in Saginaw, but that I was not sure how to make it the rest of the way home. When I told him that we were in Saginaw he asked, "Saginaw, Michigan?!" in a shocked voice? And I told him "No, Saginaw, Texas, silly". He said, (now fully awake) "What the hell are we doing at the mint?" I told him that I had no idea where we were, and I pulled up at the first place that I could find, not noticing where we had pulled up at! He said, "Let's get the hell out of here before we get shot!"

After Larry and I had been married for 5 years - five years of drinking and doing drugs pretty much all of the time - I finally got busted trying to buy dope from someone. My dope dealer had set me up! It took Larry two days to find out where I was being held. Larry and his mother paid an attorney $30,000 to defend me and got me out on bail, but I got put on bond probation and ended up getting a dirty UA and got my bond revoked, and I was put back in jail until it was time for me to go to court. Larry came to see me on visitation every week until I was sentenced, and he made sure that I always had money on my books. I felt bad because Larry asked me the day that I got busted not to go. I told him that it would be the last time I would try to hook someone up, but that I felt that I had to go as I had promised the person that I was getting it for that I would get it, and I was a woman of my word! If I just would have listened to him, I would not have gotten locked up, or at least not right then. I was given two 10-year sentences in spite of the fact that Larry had gotten me an attorney.

The reason I got so much time was because I was a habitual offender. I was told that I got lucky with the amount of time that I was given, and I was warned that if I got into any more trouble ever, I would get an automatic 25-99 years no matter what the charge is. During the last year of my four and a half years in TDCJ, I was sent to the Hobby Unit in Marlin, Texas and "due to overcrowding", I was put into the faith-based dorm. (The faith-based dorm is a dorm allotted for spiritually-driven rehabilitation... to teach incarcerated men, women and youth about God and how they can change their lives through Christ, which is supported by a church/ministry and the programs are run by those volunteers. Mine was run Discipleship Unlimited. In the faith-based dorms, we took classes, had praise and worship, worked on substance abuse and much more.) They called the faith-based dorm their "overflow"! The time that I spent in the faith-based dorm was the time where I made the most change in myself. After so many years of trying to get into the Kairos program, I was finally accepted. The Kairos is a ministry that provides a 40-hour weekend retreat where inmates can experience God's love in a very tangible way finding forgiveness and healing. It is amazing and there is always a long waiting list to participate.

Chapter Six: Freedom and Healing

HOPE

Today is a new day that God has granted especially for you,
Remember, no matter your trials, God will always help you make
it through.
You know that God loves you and He wants what is best,
But like a teacher, sometimes He will put you through a
Test,

All you have to do is keep the faith and always stay strong,
If you keep your faith, you can't go wrong.
Stay strong in your faith and always wear your armor, in all
that you do,
Because if you don't - you know that Satan will be all over
You!
All that God asks of you is to be the best Christian that
you can possibly be,
And promise that we will do all that God asks of you and
Me.
I thank God for even the smallest things in this world of
Ours,
Such as the birds, the bees and all the beautiful
flowers.

In my third year of doing my time, my aunt wrote me a letter telling me that my mother was dying. She had two aneurysms that were inoperable. They said that they did not expect her to live much longer. I had to come to terms with this information and I needed to figure out what to do about the strained relationship with my mom. I had, thankfully, been in touch with my oldest daughter Mary and with my son, and we were in good standing by the grace of God. I spoke with my friend and "bunkie" (cell mate), Tina, who I had become close to, and I spoke to a faith-based dorm volunteer who I had also become close to about my mother. I had to do a lot of praying with others and praying by myself. I finally came to the conclusion, that if I were truly going to do my best to live as a Christian, then I would have to let go of all of the past grudges and anger if I were to have any chance at all to grow. Not only that, but how could I possibly ask my own children to forgive me for my past mistakes if I could not give my forgiveness to my parents for what they had done to me?! So, I wrote a letter to my mother, and I asked her for her forgiveness for anything that I may have done in the past to hurt her, and I told her that I forgave her for all that she had done to hurt me!

Next, I had to write the hardest letter in my life... I had to write my father and give him forgiveness as well. My father had Alzheimer's, so I wrote him a letter and I prayed, and I gave it to God, and I tore it up and threw it in the trash! For the first time in my life, I felt totally free.

I wrote a letter to my husband Larry and I told him that he had to make a choice between the dope and me. I told him that when I got home that I wanted us to start going to church. I told him that I could no longer live the lifestyle that I had lived for over 30 years and that I was getting too old to do time. By the grace of God, he chose me over the drugs.

When I got out of prison, I went through many changes, and people took advantage of me because I was a felon and because I did not have a Social Security card. I took a job at a discount mart and I worked 12-14 hours a day for $20 a day. I had to work there for six months before I found another one. One of the best things that happened after my release was that I went to a retreat that was hosted by a prison ministry named <u>Discipleship Unlimited</u>.

Reignite is a group that meets once a year in April, and we all get together for 3 days, and it's made up of men and women who had graduated from the faith-based dorms in TDCJ and continued to follow God upon their release. We would spend our time there updating each other on our lives, do praise and worship and visit and we would break up in groups and do activities and have drawings for prizes and a lot more. It is always such a treat to see everyone after a year of being apart. We also encourage those who have fallen or have been struggling in their lives and try to help get them back on track. I love going to Reignite every year. I look forward to it all year, as I get to see a lot of the volunteers that put their hearts and a lot of hard work into the faith-based dorms and into helping us change our lives. We also get to see Linda Strom who started Discipleship Unlimited and the faith-based dorms in TDCJ, and whom many of us consider a mother.

Another person who I look forward to seeing every year is Carla Hooton who is the administrator of the faith-based dorms. She is an awesome lady and she also puts all her heart into the ministry.

Not long after going to Reignite, I got a call from my aunt Joy telling me that if I wanted to see my mother alive again, that I had better hurry, as they did not expect her to live much longer. My mother had held on for a couple of years in pain, just so she could see me one more time before she died. What was I going to do? We were barely getting by and I had just got out of prison, so it would not be easy to get parole to allow me to go. So, I called my good friend, Merry, and I told her the situation, and I told her that it was important to me to be able to make peace with my mother before she dies. She told me that her and her husband could help me with a few bucks as a tithe. I called everyone that I knew and a lot of them chipped in, and the people of my home church also helped to get me the money that I needed to fly to Idaho and see my mother, as well as the funds to stay in a motel for 3 days and a little money for food. Next, I called my parole officer, Mrs. Dutch, and I told her what was going on and how very important it was that I get a chance to see my mother before she dies. She said that she would do what she could, but that she did not think that they would allow me to go, since I had not been out of prison for very long. I prayed, and I asked God to please help me find a way to go see my mother, so that she could die in peace knowing that I was clean and okay! I told God that if it is His will, please let me be able to go see my mother one last time. By the grace of God, in three days, my parole officer got the necessary permission for me to go see my mother! I got enough money to go see her, and my dear friend Merry made all of the arrangements for me to go! God is so good and faithful! When I arrived in Boise, Idaho, where my mother was, a bus took me to my hotel and next to the hotel was a hospital, and I went to the hospital gift shop and I bought my mother some clean socks, a devotional book for women, and some candy, and a stuffed animal. I would sit by my mother's side and read to her, and I would talk to her for a while, until it was time for my mother to go eat. My mother could not feed herself so one of the aides that worked there asked me if I wanted to feed her? I told her sure, that I had never done it, but that it would be my pleasure to do so. I went to feed her, and she put her head down and began to cry. I put my finger under her chin and I held her head up and I smiled, and I said, "Don't be ashamed, Mama, you fed me when I was a baby and I needed help to eat, so allow me to have the pleasure and the honor to help you eat"! So, my mother allowed me to feed her, and I told her that I loved her.

The next day before I left to come back to Texas, I sat by my mother's bed, and I told her that she was the best mother she could be under the circumstances and that I was clean for the first time in 30 years, and I promised her that I would never again go back to the life I used to live. I told her that I loved her, with tears running down my face, as I knew I would never again see my mother alive. I wasted so many years being angry and bitter and refusing to forgive my mother and try to work things out with her. I had received a call from an aunt the night before I went to see my mother for the last time, and she told me that I needed to tell my mother that it was okay for her to let go. I asked why I had to be the one to tell her that it was okay to let go? She said because my mother held on for a couple of years in pain so that she could say goodbye to me, so I needed to be the one to tell her that it was okay to let go if she was tired and in pain. It was the hardest thing that I have had to do in such a long time. So, before I said goodbye to my mother, I held up her face and I asked her if she knew that I loved her? She nodded her head with tears running down her face as she could not speak. I told her,

"Look Mama, I am clean now, after 30 years of using drugs I am drug free and I give you my word that I will never again do drugs or live that life!" I told her that I knew that she was tired and really wanted to let go, and if she could not do it anymore, it was okay for her to let go. I told her that we made peace with one another and that I am going to be fine now. So, with a heavy heart I said goodbye to my mother and then prepared to go back home to Texas.

As I sat in the hotel lobby thinking about my mother and my trip and praying that my mother would no longer have to suffer, I began speaking to one of the employees of the hotel and came to find out, ALL the hotel employees were ex-cons and recovering addicts. We were talking all through the night, and it just amazed me to learn that not only were the employees of the hotel ex-cons and recovering addicts, but a lot of the people staying there were as well! I do not believe in accidents; I believe that God allowed me to see this so that it would give me hope for the future!

I got back home and went back to work at the store, and about a week after I left Idaho, my daughter Mary called me, and she said "Mom, I am sorry to tell you this, but Nana passed away this morning." I began crying and I told her thank you for being the one to call me! My boss suggested for me to leave and go home so that I could deal with the grief of losing my mother. So, I called Larry and told him that I had just been informed that my mother had passed away, and I needed him to come and get me. Before my mother died, I had written her a poem and a letter, and I had called my Aunt and told her I needed to get an address to send it to. I read her the letter and the poem on the phone, and she said, "No, don't send it because I don't think that it will get here before she dies." So, my aunt had me read both a little at a time, so she could write it down and read it to her for me. I was told that my mother heard both before she died and then they read it at her celebration of life ceremony, as they did not want to cry over the ending of her life but rather celebrate the life that she had lived! My aunt said that when she read them to my mom that my mom had tears running down her face. The letter that I wrote my mother before she died is as follows...

Mom,

     I will always remember the times we went on long walks together, so you could lose weight, and then we would go to the cafe and eat a cinnamon roll. You would laugh and say it was like cutting off your nose to spite your face. I will always remember riding horses with you, playing freeze tag together and the memory of sharing the birth of my first-born child together. We have shared many such good times together Mom. I shall always remember you as the beautiful and courageous woman you were when I saw you at Valley View.

     It was both a blessing and a gift to spend quality time with you @ Valley View and reading to you out of the Women's Prayer book about mother's, and seeing you smile when I gave you a few small gifts or when I was able to give you a few hugs and kisses. I will treasure your laughter when I reminded you of the time when Perry got sprayed by a skunk! The last time I saw you Mom, I did not see a poor, pathetic woman in a chair, I saw my beautiful mother who was very courageous and strong and who shared 3 wonderful days with me.

     Thank you, Mom. You gave me a wonderful and priceless gift, one of which I will never forget. I am NOT saying goodbye but see you later!!!

That was the letter that I wrote her before she died and that my aunt was kind enough to write it down and read it to her. And she had been right, my mother would not have lived long enough for it to have arrived in the mail....

    It was not long after losing my mother that my family and I suffered another loss. You see, a few months later our house burned down and my mother-in-law (Ruby) did not have insurance on the house, so we lost everything! My mother-in-law had recently had a pacemaker put in and then the house fire. We had no money and we did not know what we were going to do or where we were going to go. It was going to be very hard to find a place to live as a lot of places won't rent to a felon. Then the matter of where we were going to take Ruby until we could figure out what we were going to do.... At the time I was working through a Temp Service, and I had to go to work that day, and Larry had so much on his mind with worrying about his mom and what we were going to do with her, etc. A friend of ours agreed to allow Ruby to stay at his house for a short time, and the Red Cross helped us to get a Motel room for three days and a change of clothes. Ruby's poor dog died in the house fire as it had crawled under the bed to get away from the smoke and it died under the bed. The room in which Larry and I stayed was left unburned, so we continued to stay in our room.

One morning, very early in the morning, when it was almost time for me to go to work, the house caught on fire again! This time, the house was totally destroyed, and we lost another one of our dogs in the house fire, as she crawled under the house to get away from the fire, as she got spooked by the fire. We could not get her to come out from under the house, and I thought that I was going to lose Larry, as I would call out to him and he did not answer. I got on my knees and I started crying hysterically and begging God not to allow me to lose my husband. I was so thankful when he finally came out carrying our other dog Lucy Lou!!! After the second house fire, we could no longer stay in our room behind the garage because we could no longer keep power on at our house. After the first house fire, my mother-in-law was determined that the house could be saved, though it was nothing but charcoal and I secretly prayed that it could not be saved. Be careful what you pray for, as prayer from one of God's children are powerful and His answers come in many forms! The Red Cross came out to the scene of both house fires, and when they saw where it was, they said, "We have to stop meeting like this!"

Larry and I were wondering the streets looking for a place to rent and we were at wits end; we were turned down everywhere we went. No one wanted to rent to a felon. As we wondered the streets in our truck trying to find a place to live, I began to pray asking God to help us find a place to live! Just as I finished praying, good friends of ours - Catherine and her husband Chris - saw us and started honking their horn and told us to pull over. They asked us where we were going to go? I told her that we didn't know as everywhere we go, they did not want to let us rent from them because I was a felon. Some people suggested that my husband Larry and my mother-in-law get a place under their names and then I could sneak in; it is done all the time they said. But you see, I had started a new life, and I was trying my hardest to live the right way! I had to have faith in the Lord and trust that God is going to take care of the situation. Plus, truly, I did not want to get into a place under false pretenses and then someone finds out that I lied, and then we would be back in the same spot we were in before. So, Catherine and Chris told us that they had been thinking for a long time about moving into another place and they felt like the time had come to make the change, and there was an apartment up the street from their house that they wanted. At the same time, the people who were allowing my mother-in-law to stay with them had gotten tired of having her there, but did not want to hurt Larry's feelings, so they said that we needed to find somewhere else to take her as his kids were moving back in and there just was not enough room for her and them. So, Chris and Catherine said that we could stay at the house with them until they were able to move out, and they had already made arrangements with the landlady for us to take over the rent of their house. Larry's aunt allowed my mother-in-law to stay with her for a couple of weeks until Chris and Catherine could move into their new place. Chris and Catherine were a blessing to us during this hard time.

They came after the first fire and brought boxes and tape to try and pack up the things that we were able to save and spent endless hours helping us to pick through the rubble.

Larry and I were so blessed in many ways during this trying time. We were given money from friends such as my Awesome friend Merry and her husband Dino, and our church family helped us with donations, and our dear friend Alice Hoffman came to the rescue and allowed my mother-in-law to stay with her for a short time as well, and she tried to help us recover whatever we could from the rubble alongside Catherine , Larry , Chris and I.... Anyway, approximately a week later Larry, Ruby and I had a house once again and we began to pick up the pieces. I was still working through PDQ Temporaries and Catherine again, was a blessing as I rode with her to work in the mornings and Larry would pick me up in the afternoons.

I worked at the same place for quite a while, then I got upset with the boss and I quit. For a while I bounced back and forth from one warehouse to another. I was working at a warehouse that worked on cell phones and I met a woman there who I had become friends with, and she asked me if I would be willing to clean her house for money, and since I was not working at the time I agreed to help her get her house cleaned up.

I ended up falling from a 7-foot ladder and I broke my heel in two places. When I fell, I tried to get her and her husband to take me to the hospital, but they tried to convince me that my heel was only sprained and wanted to take me home. I told them that I was sure that it was broken and not sprained, and I had to crawl to the couch and get on it by myself. I finally talked them into taking me to the hospital where it was confirmed that my heel was indeed broken. I asked my friend and her husband to please help me with the medical bills, because I could not afford the bills that would come from breaking my heel. They said that they did not have any money to give me. I told them that I did not want to sue them, that I just wanted to get some help with the medical bills. They insisted that they did not have any money to give me.

I knew that it was going to be costly to heal so I felt that I did not have any choice but to hire an attorney. I had to find a pro-bono attorney and they had pity on me because of my situation and agreed to help me. The sad thing is, because I was a felon they said, that it would work against me. I asked them how it would work against me and they said though it was not fair, my past would hurt me in court because a lot of felons try to pull cons on people, so they don't have to get a job, and therefore a jury wouldn't trust that it was an accident. It seemed so unfair that even the legal system won't let us forget about past mistakes! This accident had nothing to do with the fact that I was a felon. I think the only thing that helped me was the fact that I had worked all my life which could be proven and that I had never filed a lawsuit against anyone in my life. It would take over a year for me to get any money from my suit and we had to settle out of court to get that, as my attorney said that he was not sure that I would get anything, if we took it to court in front of a jury because of my felonies. When all was said and done, all I got out of my suit after court costs and lawyer fees and the $7,000 hospital bill was $4,000!

I was unable to work for months and was in extreme pain, with a foot that will never be the same, and I was very disappointed by the outcome. It was quite some time before I would be able to go back to work.

I started out helping my friend, Merry, out at the Dollar Tree in Rockwall as they needed help, because it was time for inventory, and they were shorthanded, and Merry asked if I could go help her out. I would stay with her and her husband Dino while I was working there because it was too far for me to go back and forth to my house in Fort Worth. I always love spending time at Merry and Dino's house as they always make me feel both welcome and special while I am there! I like the fact that my friend Merry knows, that if I am able to help with something, then I am more than willing to do so. I am glad that she feels comfortable in asking for my help. Merry, Dino, and I have done a lot of things together and it always makes me feel good. One of those things that we did together was go to Reignite. Anyway, Merry and Dino have been a blessing in my life, and I love them very much. Merry is such an awesome friend. Merry, my friend Tina, and my friend DeAnne have formed a group with just the four of us that we call "Sister Chicks For Christ", and I had the idea of having matching shirts made that have our names in the front, and in the back it says " Sister Chicks For Christ " and has a cross in the middle, which our very talented friend and Sister-in-Christ, Tina, made even better by putting rhinestones around the cross. Then we had a cap with a cross on it with the same rhinestones around the cross. Merry, Tina, and DeAnne and I have had many great Sister's days out. We share our birthdays together. Tina and I have gone to Refuel which is a part of Reignite together. And Tina, DeAnne, Merry and I all spent time together with my daughter Mary when she came to visit.

Merry, Dino, DeAnne and I all went to Six Flags together and it was such fun. It was the first time I had gone, and it was around Christmas time. It was in 2016 and it was my second Christmas home from prison. Merry, Dino, Tina and I all went to help DeAnne when she needed help to move. These people are family to me and have been such a source of spiritual and moral support, financial support, and lots of love! I don't think there is anything that we would not do for one another if we need something. We do life together in Jesus' Name and it's great! Merry and I did time together on one prison unit and Tina and I were bunkies on another unit. I am so thankful that the four of us (actually five of us as we can't forget George who is Tina's husband and Dino which is Merry's husband) are like a family and we (me, Merry, and Tina) have grown close together since our release.

I was thankful to have Tina by my side when I was given an award at a special banquet from parole. My awesome Parole Officer, Mrs. Dutch, nominated me for the award for doing such a good job on parole. Mrs. Dutch is another awesome person that God has placed in my life. She has been supportive of my going back into prison, to speak to other women in prison, to encourage them to change their lives and to show them that it is possible to change your life if you want. I was blessed enough to be invited by Discipleship Unlimited founder Linda Strom to go into the prison and speak. As I am still on parole till 2020, I must have the permission of my Parole office and my parole officer to be allowed to go into prison. Thankfully, they support me in doing this and I am thankful. There should be more parole officers like Mrs. Dutch then maybe there would be more success stories of those who make parole. She is firm yet fair, and when she sees that her parolees are trying to better themselves, she will do anything that she can to help them! Lord only knows that she has been a Godsend many times since my release from prison, and the best thing is that she has faith in me and my ability to do better in my life, and she believes in my change. A good parole officer can mean the difference in whether a parolee makes it or not. I have had many bad parole officers in my past that just took a look at my thick file and decided before they even met me that I was going to fail like I had before. Mrs. Dutch is the first one who did not judge me because it was not my first time in prison. Mrs. Dutch, and my friends and I have all shared in many of my trials and tribulations since my release and to be honest, I don't know how well I would have done without these awesome people in my life. God has placed so many wonderful people in my life and somehow, we have all been a source of love, strength and courage to one another and we are only getting started.

We are going to continue to grow both in our individual lives and in our united lives together. I will soon be going back into prison with Merry, Tina, and DeAnne and this will be the first time that the four of us have been inside together. One time I went into prison, with my husband Larry and it was at Christmas time, and we were helping to deliver Christmas presents to the inmates and to talk with them and to pray with them, and my husband told me later that it did his heart good to see that these women were glad to see us there. It was his first time ever going into prison, as he had never been in trouble with the law, though he had done drugs for many years. It was an eye-opening experience for him.

I am going to end this part of my story for now, but before I go, let me just say that the most important thing for you to do if you are in prison or you are struggling in an addiction or whatever the case may be... is to not lose hope! Reach out to your higher power and hold onto that faith in your higher power! With God in your life, you will be amazed how He transforms you and your life into something awesome and meaningful - and **you can change**!!! It is NEVER too late to change your life if you truly want to change your life. Trust me when I say, it is amazing how many people will reach out to help you and guide you when you are ready to change. But you have to make those changes for yourself and not for someone else. It is not easy to change your way of living after having lived the same way for so long. There will be many struggles and trials and tribulations and a lot of moments when you will tell yourself that life was much easier when you were doing drugs, etc. But the trials and tribulations serve a purpose as well, they will challenge you to be strong, and make you stronger with every success that you have.

And remember, you are not alone, God is always with you. And once you have made up your mind to change, and you find a home church and build relationships there, they will help you. My family had pretty much given up on me over 30 years ago and decided that I was a lost cause. They would not have anything to do with me and when I got out of prison this time, my fourth time, and they saw that I had truly changed - they welcomed me back with open arms.

You see, when I got out of prison this time, and they told me that if I wanted to see my mother alive again that I better hurry and get to Idaho, and I jumped a bunch of hoops to make it there to see my mom... that was a test (which I did not know at the time)... to see if I would even try to go see her or if I would just decide that there was no way I could find a way to go and give up! I showed them by going to Idaho that I had changed. I did everything humanly possible to get to Idaho to go see my mother. They saw that it was not just empty words and that I had truly changed. My husband and I went to the last family reunion last year, and I saw family whom I had not seen in many years, and they all told me how proud they were of me and how much they loved me! I cannot tell you how awesome it felt to have my family love me again and tell me how proud they were of me. But it would not have been possible without God's help, and the love and support of friends and family! Cut yourself a break and stay strong knowing that anything is possible if you keep God first.

AFTERWORD

Family, Friends, and Ministry

My Family

my father, my sister Jacque, my brother John, me, and my brother Perry

My Husband, Larry

This is my husband Larry and his kids(as he could not have kids of his own) left: Lucylou, who we have had since she was born-middle: Jake, who we took from a couple who had adopted him and then decided that they did not want him-right: Cocoa, who we got from a friend.

This picture is my wedding picture 13 years ago this June 23rd!

This was the happiest day of my life and my husband has stood by me through good and bad. He stood by me while I was in prison for 4 and a half years, and he has comforted me through MANY tears and he rescued me from a very bad relationship. When we first met we shared a drug addiction but now we both share a drug free life with God as the head of our household and of our lives! We have had his mother with us since his father passed away in 2007 and we lived in her home and for the last 6 years she has lived in our home. But all together we have had her with us for going on 13 years. Larry loves his mother very much and does the best he can to be a good son to her. She is now 89 years old and can at times be very difficult but, she is his mother and she will be with us until her dying day! Larry works very hard to keep a roof over our heads though his health is not the best. My darling husband recently bought me a house and he continues to find ways to show me how much he loves me. He not only allowed my oldest sister to come live with us, but he basically supported her between jobs and he did his best to make her feel welcome. I have truly been blessed with the husband I have! He is good to me and to my kids and he and my oldest daughter Mary get alone very well!

Mama

This is a picture of my beautiful mother and my sister Jacque and brother John and my sister Jessica before mama died! Rest in peace mama, I miss you so much! I wish my brother Perry and I could have been there to take a picture with mama and my brother and sisters! This was the last picture that they had with mama before she died!

I would like to start with my mother in honor of her memory. She was the best mother that she could be under the circumstances considering the tyrant she was married to! Though there were many bad memories with my mother, there were also many good memories with her. When I was little, I remember one time when my mother tried to keep us kids out of my father's hair and decided to play freeze tag with us kids. Mama slipped and fell, and she sprang her ankle. Boy was my father ever mad. He told her not to expect him to take her to the emergency room when she would not have gotten hurt had she not been playing like a child! Of course, he did take her to the hospital, but he was not very happy about it. I remember another time when she fell and broke her leg while roller skating. When we lived on the hill in Eagle Point, Oregon I remember we got a lot of snow and mama couldn't drive her car into town, so she said that she was going to saddle two of our horses and go to town to buy some food. I was glad that mama had chosen me to go with her. I always enjoyed any private time I could get with my mom in those days. And, I remember times when mama was trying to lose weight and she would go on some very long walks and once in a while she would take me with her. On once such occasion she and I went to the bottom of the hill and parked the car and we went walking from there to Jacksonville which was 16.0 miles(I googled it) We took a couple of trash bags with us and we filled them up with as many cans and bottles as we could find from the side of the road and when we got back to White City mama and I would trade in the cans and bottles for cash and then mama would want to go to her favorite café and eat a butterhorn (of all things!) and I remember thinking " really mama, a butterhorn of all things after walking all that way to lose weight! I remember one time when mama called and told us kids to get ready because she was going to take us to the movies when she got home. So, when I went to fix my hair, I put several ponytails in my hair and I personally thought that I looked cute. Mama, however, did not think that it was so cute, and she told me that if I was going with her, I better get all those ponytails out of my hair! That day we went to see Benji, and mama embarrassed us because she started screaming "run Benji, run "when the bad guy was chasing him. I think that everyone in the theater turned around and gave us a funny look. I wanted to hide under my seat from embarrassment. I don't think that mama was at all embarrassed and seemed to be having quite a good time. I remember one time, I wanted to bake a cake, but mama was getting ready to go to town and she said that I could not bake the cake as she would be gone, and we had a gas stove. I (being stubborn and strong headed) decided that I was going to bake the cake anyway. I waited for quite some time after she left and then started to mix the batter. I knew that it would take her a very long time to come back home as it was a long way from our house into town. I was about done mixing the batter when to my surprise, I saw mama pulling up in the driveway. I didn't know what I was going to do with that batter before mama could get into the house and see it? At the time, we had a trailer connected to the house and the trailer was our kitchen and it had a back door. So, I opened the back door and I shoved mama's only mixing bowl under the trailer full of batter. I was little then, and I had forgotten all about the batter being under the trailer. Then one day, my mother was looking for her mixing bowl and she asked my sister and I where her mixing bowl was as my sister and I took turns washing dishes. Well, by the time I found her mixing bowl it was full of crusty, molded cake batter. I told mama that I had found it but that I had no idea how it got there! Do you think that my mother believed for second that mama believed that I did not know where that bowl had been? I don't think so...

My Sister, "Jacque"

Jacque and I at Reignite, Brownwood, Texas in 2018

She and I have never really been close while we were growing up. I love my sister very much and I am sure in her own way she loves me as well. But, when we were younger, she and I never saw eye to eye. She had friends and I did not, she spent the night at the houses of her friends, and I did not have friends who I could spend the night with. She had always been jealous of me because I could use long words and she did not have as extensive of a vocabulary as I did. When mama and Dad went somewhere, they would leave me in charge even though she was a year older than me and I think that she resented it. I have always felt that my father would pit us against one another and that is why we did not get along. Anyway, one time while we were living on Shasta Street in Eagle Point, we had bunkbeds and she had the top bunk and I had the bottom bunk as I had a bed wetting problem. For some reason my sister was not home that day and I decided to climb up onto her bed and take a nap because, well she wasn't using it! Besides, I had always wondered what it would be like to be on the top bunk. She came home to find me on her bed, and she got up on the top bunk and she pushed me off! When I fell, I hit the metal part at the bottom of the bunk and hit my eyebrow. My father had to take me to the emergency room, and I had to have stitches put in on my eyebrow. She got a good spanking for having pushed me, but I had to still go to school. She was so mad that she had gotten into trouble because of me (as she saw it) she told her friends that I had gotten her in trouble and that it was all my fault because had I not been on her bed in the first place then she would not have had to push me off and she would not have gotten into trouble. So, her friends terrorized me, and they would chase me and be mean to me and they threatened to pull out my stitches. Any time that my sister got into trouble it was always my fault no matter what! I am thankful that she and I are on a friendlier basis right now, and I am thankful for the little time that we were able to share together when she came to stay at my house with my husband and me. I wish my sister well and I feel that she has a good heart, but I just wish that she had better desires for her life and would do something to change her circumstances. I would never wish anything bad on my sister, but I do get somewhat frustrated with her because I know that her life could be so much better if she would only believe that she deserved better. You see, a few years ago an aunt of mine told me that she did not think I was ever happy because in my heart I did not believe that I deserved it. I believe that for years and years, I did not think I deserved anything good because my father had convinced me that I would never be loved and that I would never make anything of myself. When your own parent says something like that, I think that any child would tend to believe it! I believe that she deserves a much better life and I only pray that one day, she too will believe that she deserves better than what she has! I love you Jill, and I pray that one day you will find the peace and happiness that you seek!

The last picture is of My Mother-In-Law Ruby Starnes, me on the left and my sister on the right after church. The picture above is of Jacque in front of a wall here in Fort Worth, Texas!

My Brother Perry

Perry and I when I went to Oregon in 2016.

Oh, my darling brother Perry, how very much I love him! Perry and I have almost always been close to one another and I think it is because we have much the same spirit. Though he may not have always liked the things I did or the way that I lived, he never stopped loving me. He always accepted me the way I was, and he never had a cross thing to say to me! I sometimes think that it was only by the grace of God that us kids didn't kill each other. We were very mean to each other and I contribute that to the fact that we were around so much violence and violence breeds violence. I remember when I would run away from home and I would get sent back I would discover that Perry had been telling some wild stories about me and my adventures away from home. I would send him some post cards from places I had been and just let him know that I was okay. Once I went to work in Mississippi planting trees for the forestry service and I sent him a card from Mississippi telling him what I was doing and where I was and that I thought he would like a card from there. He says that he still has the one from Mississippi and a few others as well. I was talking to him on the phone a little and I told him that I was writing a book about some of the people in my life and what they mean to me and some of the memories that I have with those people. I told him that one painful memory that I have with him and that was when he shot me with his BB gun that he got for Christmas one year. We were living on the hill in Eagle Point and we were out of school for summer vacation and we were so bored with nothing to do and he had his BB gun in his hand. He got an impish smile on his face and he started laughing. (It was just him and I out there at the time) and I asked him what he was laughing for? He asked me if I wanted to go hunting with him? I said sure, what are we going to hunt? He said, I am going to hunt you! So, I took off running and I told him that he better not shoot me! He kept running towards me and yelling, you better run! So, I took off running through the woods and pow, he hit me on my left hip! I was so angry that I snatched the BB gun away from him and I shot him back without aiming. He started crying and yelling and he said that he was going to tell my parents. I told him to go ahead and tell them and I would tell them that he had shot me too and that he had shot me first. He did not tell our parents and neither did I!!! But I think the best memory that I have of my brother Perry, is one time while we lived on the hill, he and my brother John were walking home from a friend's house one night and they were little. Well, you know how curious little kids are, well Perry saw something run over the hill side and he went to see what it was, and he grabbed it and it was a skunk that he had grabbed by the tail and it sprayed him in the face. My other brother said that Perry started screaming that he was blind. So, my brother John told him that he was going to get our mom and dad so they could help him. John went running home and he was screaming for help and half out of breath he explained to my parents that Perry had been sprayed by a skunk and that he said that he could not see. My father took John to see what was going on with Perry and when they found him, they brought him home. They made him sit in the back of dad's truck because he stunk so bad. Mama made him bathe in some tomato juice to try to take the smell off him but no matter how she tried she could not get rid of that smell. His eye sight did return but that smell.... My dad told him that he was going to be sleeping outside with the dogs as that smell was so bad! I love you dear brother, and you will always be special to me...

My brother Perry and my son Bobby! Everyone says that my son and my brother look a lot alike!

My Brother John

My two brothers who I love very much and wish that I lived closer so that we could share a better relationship! I wish my brothers would have grown closer together rather than farther apart! It is sad to me that they live so close in miles yet are so distant with one another!

My brother John was the youngest of the four of us and he was a very curious little boy when he was younger. Not to mention that he loved taking dares and risks and he could be ornery as ever! He and my brother Perry used to get on top of the garage and jump from the garage to the outhouse and keep going back and forth and back and forth. It would scare me to death to see them jumping back and forth like that though they had no fear! Of course, they did it without the knowledge of our parents. They sometimes went to the pond and would jump their bikes into the pond!!! I remember one-time John and I got bored and I'm not sure how it happened, but we started play tug a war with a rope and a tire that was attached to the rope. I finally got tired of playing and I let go of my rope and my brother John went flying into a barbed wire fence where he cut his lip on the left side! Boy did I ever get into trouble for that smart move. I felt bad that he had cut his lip, but my father didn't care, I still got severely punished for it! I kept telling my brother that I was sorry, and he replied, it's okay sis, it gives me character and girls like guys with scars! My brother John was generous like that, he tried so hard to make me feel better. But I also remember when he wasn't so generous and only thought about his own hide! One day for some reason, he and I stayed home from school and we got bored and we were the only ones at home. I think if I remember right, that we pretended to be sick so we would not have to go to school that day, yes, we played hooky! Anyway, John talked me into getting my mother's .22 and going over the hill and shooting it. He said that if we got caught that he would take the blame for it but that we would be back and put the .22 back before mama had a chance to get home. Dummy me, I should have realized that no matter what he said if we got caught that I would be the one more severely punished as I was the oldest and I should have known better! We took the .22 and some shells and went over the hillside from our house and we began shooting at trees and things and I think when John took the last shot a neighbor went by and saw us with the gun and heard the shot and called my mother. By the time we went to the top of the hill and got to the house my mother was parked in the driveway!!! We were scared to death and we didn't know what to do. I told my brother to remember that he had promised to take responsibility if we got caught. He said that he did not know what I was talking about and that I was the oldest and I should have known better! We decided to put the .22 under the garage and bury the shells in the ground. We went into the house pretending that we didn't know anything that had happened. The moment we stepped inside my mother asked in a very angry voice "where is my gun"? We answered in unison, what gun mama? She said, "you know what gun"!!! She sent John to go get the gun and she went to get her belt and she said "come here Mary Annette "!!! She began spanking the hell out of me and I kept trying to tell her that it had been John's idea! She said that she didn't care whose idea it had been, I was the oldest and I should have known better! Once she was done wearing the belt out on us, she sent us to bed! When my father got home, he beat us half to death! Boy, I sore the next day! I love you my dear brother John, and I miss you more than you know! I wish that you and your wife would include me more in your lives and realize that it does not matter to me what you are doing in your lives, I love you & always will! Besides John, who am I of all people to pass judgement on anyone?

This is my brother John Hulse and his beautiful wife Cheri Johnson!

I want to thank Cheri for loving my brother and for giving him the love that he needed so badly! Also, I would like to thank her for putting up with his crap because I believe that we women put up with a lot of men's crap! Lol… To my brother John I want to say that no matter what I love you and always will! You need to remember brother, that not EVERYONE will judge you for the way you choose to live your life and you need to let those who CHOOSE to be a part of your life and love you to do so! You need to stop beating yourself up bro, you have always had a good heart. I know you have had a rough life brother, but it could be full of a lot more love if you would just let it be. Once Aunt Joy told me that she thinks that the reason why I was never happy is because I did not believe that I deserved to be happy. You know brother, I think that is the way you feel. You and your lovely wife and your kids are always in my prayers and I love you very much!!! Cheri, you are a beautiful person inside and out and you also have a good heart. While I was at your house there were people who spoke highly of both you and my brother and I hope you both never let go of each other and the love that you share both for each other and for your kids. Remember, life is too short to hold on past mistakes and grudges and all it will do is make you bitter and miserable. I am NOT saying that you have grudges against one another, and we ALL make mistakes so please don't misunderstand what I am saying. I pray that if your relationship ever becomes broken (God forbid) that you can both find a way to repair it. The pictures that I have seen of both of you with your children are FULL of love and joy and I wish that for your family ALWAYS!!! I love you both very much!

My sister-in-law and two of her children. I love this picture so full of fun and love! I wish that I had such awesome memories that I share with my children!

This is a very special picture of a mother and her love for her son! I love this picture and wish that I would have had one like this with my mother. This picture of mother and son is priceless. Cheri, I know that you treasure moments like this with your children and I love to see the smiles on your faces. I pray that you will share many more memories like this with your beautiful children.

Here is my sister Jacque, mama, John is in her arms, me and my brother Perry! Is she happy in this picture?

She looks happy and all of us had smiles on our faces. It makes me wonder how and when everything turned sour for our family! I have several good memories of mama, I remember the times when she used to try to keep peace between my father and us kids, when she would play freeze tag with us or take us roller skating or the trips that we would take to Touvelle Park in Oregon and let us go down the rapids on an innertube. I remember once when Mama took us to the movies to see Benji. Mama was a very emotional woman and when

Benji was being chased by the bad guys Mama began to loudly scream "run Benji, run"! I think that everyone in the theater looked at mama in a funny way as if she had suddenly grown horns on her head. I wanted to hide under my seat with embarrassment! Mama had a thing for soap operas, and she watched them every single day.

I think that she lived vicariously through the people on those soaps. I remember when Mama and I went on a long walk from White City, Oregon to Jacksonville, Oregon (according to google, it is 12.9 miles) and during this long walk, we collected cans and bottles in trash bags so that we could turn them in for money upon our return to White City. After we got back to White City, we traded all our cans and bottles and went to the Roadrunner Café where we bought Butter horns. I remember laughing and shaking my head because the whole purpose for our walk was so that Mama could exercise and lose weight and here, we are eating a very fattening Butter horn! Another thing that I will always remember about Mama, is that every year we went over the hill on our property on her birthday to pick out a Christmas tree!

Mama would always pick just the right tree and we would spend the day decorating the tree. It smelled of fresh evergreen in our house and it was a lot of fun to decorate the tree. I remember us kids looking for mistletoe so that we could try to take it to town and sell it. I think we thought that we were going to get rich selling mistletoe. One thing about it, there was plenty of it on that hill.

I remember one time when Mama told me that the Indians used to eat cat tails, so I decided to taste one and I bit into it and got a mouth full of fuzzy stuff! I told Mama that I thought she had said that the Indians used to eat them? She started laughing and she said that she meant that they used to eat the roots! I thought that I was never going to get all that fuzzy stuff out of my mouth. And another thing that I think about is when my brother Perry got sprayed in the face by a skunk while he and my brother John were on their way home from a friend's house and John had to go get my father to help Perry. Perry was screaming that he was blind, and dad made him sit in the back of the truck because he stunk so bad. Mama tried to wash him in Tomato Juice to try and rid him of that awful smell! God almighty how he stunk! But try as she might, she could not get rid of that terrible smell! Another time that makes me both laugh and smile is when while we were living on the hill, Perry snuck behind the outhouse and he put on a boogeyman hat and he waited for Mama to come out to the bathroom and he was going to try to scare her. It was dark outside as it was late at night and the light from the shed made his shadow cast him as a big person. Mama started screaming but nobody heard her, and she came running into the house out of breath! Perry came into the house and was laughing his butt off! Mama told him he was lucky she did not have a weapon because she would have beat him to death!

I shall always treasure and cherish all these memories with my mother, and many more!

My Beloved Children

Mama and my son, Bobby, when he was younger . Mama loved her grandchildren, and this is one of the few pictures that I have of mama and my son. I think that it was taken at my Aunt's Ranch? Everyone says that my son looks a lot like my brother Perry. I am glad that mama had a chance to spend some time with her grandson. When my son was born, I had named him Harvey Glenn after my Grandfather whom I never had a chance to meet as he met a tragic death when my mother was little. Once his father got custody of him, he changed his name to Robert Newborn Ford. It made me both angry and sad when I found out that his father had changed his name!

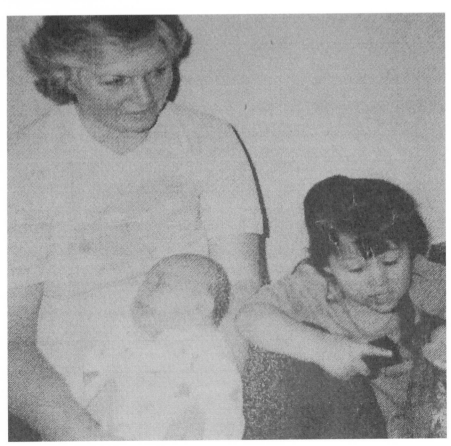

Mama and my son and my daughter Mary were little, and my son was first born! Mary was so protective of her little brother!

My Grandma Hulse and my daughter Mary and me

My daughter Mary

Mary and my son Bobby (I had named my son Harvey Glenn after my mother's father and once his father got custody he changed his name to Bobby.).

This is the most recent picture of my daughter Mary and I when she came to Fort Worth, Texas to see me.

The most recent photo that I have of my son Bobby.

I did not include any photos of my youngest daughter because she does not have anything to do with me and I wish to respect her privacy and do not wish to cause a bigger rift between my daughter and I. My oldest daughter Mary lives in the state of Oregon and my son lives in the state of Colorado. My youngest daughter does not wish to believe that I have changed in a positive way. It breaks my heart because I have truly changed my life and I live my life for the Lord now. I have come to the understanding that if it is meant for her and I to have a relationship of any kind it will have to be in God's time and not in mine! None the less, I love all of my children very much and I am thankful that not all of them have left me in the past! Though I love all of my children, I am especially thankful for my daughter Mary and her faith in my ability to change for the better, for all of her love and support and for wanting me to be a continuous part of her life! Thank you Mary, your faith in me and your love for me means the world to me! You have been a constant source of encouragement and strength to me.

Extended Family

I am going to start this section with a woman who was always near and dear to my heart! Below, you will see a picture of her, my Granny! Granny was such a wonderful woman and to me a lot of times she was my place of refuge! I remember one summer I spent it with my Granny. She was always so loving, and she loved her grandchildren very much! I think my granny knew that I had it the hardest at home and she would let me go spend the summer at her house in Idaho City, Idaho. She would call me her little pea picker as she had a garden in

her back yard with peas, onions, beets, potatoes (of course) strawberries, and many other things and she would have me help her in the garden. She was sweet and kind yet strict in her ways. I remember one time she let me ride her three-wheel bicycle and she gave me a warning not to go down the hill by the side of her house as if traffic came, I could get seriously hurt or killed. So, what did I do? Yep, you guessed it, I took the bicycle up that hill and began ridding it down the hill and sure enough, cars came from every direction and I could not stop so I turned the handlebars and went into her neighbors barbed wire fence and landed with the bike on top of me! Boy was she mad at me! She started yelling (once she knew I was okay) Mary Annette, what did I tell you about going down that hill on my bike? Do you realize that you could have been killed? Oh, how that broke my heart to have my granny so mad at me. I think that I had just scared her to death. Another time that I recall making her mad at that same visit is one day I was outside, and I was board and I found some cat tails, so I pulled them apart and wet down my granny's car and I began to put the fuzzy stuff inside of them all over her car! Yep, windows and all! When granny saw it, she was furious! So, granny told me to clean up her car and then to meet her in the house. She had gathered a bunch of cat tails and some pipe cleaners, some crayons, and tooth picks and she taught me how to make some animals out of them. She had a few lady friends there in Idaho City, and they would allow me to stack their firewood for them and they would give me cookies and hot cocoa and they would pay me for helping them! I would hide all the money that I made that summer under my granny's rug so that no one could steal it from me. I don't know who I thought was going to steal my money, but I just felt it necessary to hide it. When it came time for me to go back home, I couldn't remember where I hid it. My granny was a librarian for awhile and a switchboard operator though I am not sure if she was both at the same time or not? I used to thank it was so cool for her to be a switchboard operator out of her own house. I remember going to the library sometimes with her and reading while she took care of her library stuff. I used to love going to the library with granny, and she loved books so much. I remember that my granny used to read a book, smoke a cigarette and drink a small glass of wine before she went to sleep at night. Oh, and could my granny ever cook! She could make left overs taste like a gourmet meal. She cooked on a wood burning stove and it tasted better than any food I had ever eaten in my life. My granny also like classical music and she listened to it before bed while reading her poetry and drinking her wine! I always felt so loved at my granny's house and I felt wanted and understood. I used to wish that I could move in with my granny. My granny used to write poetry and I would like to think that my love for her had something to do with my writing poetry. I miss you very much granny, may you rest in peace with mama.

A switchboard much like the one granny used!
This one is in a museum in Idaho City, Idaho

Granny's House. Larry at one of our visits. I took these pictures while I was visiting Idaho City, Idaho last year! It saddened me to see her yard in such a way! Granny took such good care of her yard! Above you will also see a picture of a switchboard that is much like the one that my granny had in her house when she was a switchboard operator! You will also see a picture of a wood stove that looks like the one that granny used to use when she cooked!

Aunt Donna

My Aunt Donna and her family

Taken in Idaho, 2016

Both pictures have "Jimmy" the skunk that my Aunt Donna had when I was a kid. When I first met Jimmy, it was quite startling! I think that Aunt Donna spoiled him like she would a child! Lol…

My Aunt Donna's beautiful yard

My Dear Uncle Art

My cousin Janet Shira

My cousins Pat, son Mike and David

This beautiful little girl is my cousin Pat's grand-daughter by his daughter Rachel and her name is Piper! I have only had the pleasure of meeting this beautiful girl once!

Jorden (left) and Arther (right) are my cousin Pat's grandsons by his son, Mike. So adorable!

This handsome fellow is my cousin Pat's Grandson and is also his son Mike's son

My Friends

Joyce Delaney

I would like to start this chapter with my dear friend Joyce Delaney! I met her through a pen pal program through her church. Though from the beginning I knew that it was a God thing that we had met at all! You see, she lives in New Jersey and I was in prison in the state of Texas! How my name reached her over the miles I may never know. But when this Angel sent to me by the Lord above entered into my life, my life changed forever and for the better. Before she came into my life, I had already been hurt a lot by people who I had written to. They would find out that I was locked up for drugs and that I had a long criminal history and they would write me off! I already had selfesteem issues, and I did not think that I could handle anymore rejections. So, the first letter that I wrote her I told her that I was going to tell her the worst of the worst about me and if she decided not to write me back that I would understand and I proceeded to tell her ALL that there was to know about me! I was sure that I would not hear from her again. Imagine my surprise when I did get a letter from her and she wanted to get to know me!!! The second thing that told me that it was a gift from God for me to get to know her was because I had told her that one of my most favorite thing to watch on tv as a child was The Nancy Drew Hardy Boys Mysteries! The next thing I know, she was sending me a greeting card that looked like a book cover and it was of The Nancy Drew Hardy Boys Mysteries!!! Since that first letter from this dear lady, I have grown in leaps and bounds. I told her in a letter that someone wanted ME to go to a Vocational Landscaping class and that they actually thought that I was smart enough to pass it! Yea right, me? She immediately wrote me back telling me that she had faith in me and that she thought that I should do it! Her faith in me (which no one has ever had in me) made me decide to take the course and I PASSED IT! After that I knew that I could do anything that I put my mind to. Through her, I learned to love myself for the first time in all my life. She helped me in so many ways, probably more than she will ever know! We are still in touch today and I will always have a special place in my heart for her. She gave me love, faith in myself and she has taught me so much! I love you very much Joyce, and you will always be my special angel!

Dino & Merry Fuller

My special friends Merry and Dino Fuller (and their awesome dog, Tiger)

Dino, Merry and Tiger Fuller have become like family to me! They are MUCH more than just friends. Merry and Dino were an endless source of comfort and help to my family and I when our house burned to the ground. Merry and I were in prison together for a short time and even then Merry was very kind to me. Merry was a lot of help and support to me when my mother passed away. She helped by making all of the necessary reservations for me and she gave me a lot of love and support. She spent time with me and my daughter Mary was here visiting me and she has always been there to make me feel like I belong. Merry and Dino are two of the kindest people that I know. They have been a true blessing in my life as has Tiger who I love and adore! They are both very talented in singing and playing music and they love God with all of their hearts. One of the many things that I like about Merry is that she is not afraid to tell it like it is!!!

George and Tina Washington

George and Tina as chaperones at their daughter's Highschool Prom.

Tina speaking at a luncheon.

My dear friend Tina, I love her so very much! She has been a source of inspiration, strength reinforces my faith! Tina truly amazes me with her ability to maneuver all the things that she does. She does so much for so many and still manages to further herself and to accomplish so much! I just don't know how she does it. She helps many people in many ways and has accomplished so much since her release from prison. She is an inspirational speaker, she goes into prison and speaks on how God has changed her life, she is a seamstress and clothing designer, a mother, a wife and an Author just to name a few of her accomplishments.

She is truly an amazing and strong woman who can and will succeed in all that she sets out to accomplish! Lets not forget that she also has her own show on Facebook and she makes prom dresses for those who can not afford one. Somehow she still finds time to help me when I need it and she always makes time for me even when free time is a luxury that Tina does not have. She found an awesome man to marry by the name of George Washington and together they are unstopable!

George supports Tina in all that she does and you can tell that they love each other very much. While my sister was living with my husband and I, Tina made my sister feel comfortable and was very kind to her. She was very sweet to my daughter when she came as well. Tina has made outfits for me for special events like she made a beautiful dress for my first birthday out of prison and she and her mother took me out to eat for my birthday. Tina and George and my husband and I have our anniversaries close together so we try to celebrate them together and we are more like family than friends. Tina was the first one to not only welcome me into the Faithbase Dorm in TDCJ but she helped me as I could barely walk as I had been injurred.

Tina talked me into taking a stand in faith in TDCJ and put in to become part of KAIROS as I was not even going to try for it as I had tried when I was in prison 3 times before and was never accepted. Tina told me that I needed to have faith in God and take a step in faith and sign up for it. So I did and I made it!!! Tina was there for me when I was presented with an award from parole and she has been an awesome friend. God certainly must have a special place reserved for Tina in heaven!!!

DeAnne Barber

This beautiful lady is a very special friend of mine and I have learned a lot from her! She serves God with a full heart and has such a great love of the Lord! I will not say much about her as she is also a very private person and I must respect that! I have spent many hours with DeAnne and I would like to think that we have learned from each other.

DeAnne has come a long ways since I met her as have I. I was thankfully introduced to her by Merry and Dino Fuller and then I introduced her and Merry to Tina. The difference between DeAnne and Tina, Merry and I is that DeAnne has never been to prison, or at least not in the same respect as the rest of us have been. You see, DeAnne is a servant of the Lord by being involved in Prison Ministry so we all knew her from when she used to go to the prison while we were there. Now, we are friends out here in the free world and the 4 of us follow the Lord together!

DeAnne is a woman of great beauty both inside and out, and she has such a great heart for the Lord. I am not going to go into too much detail about DeAnne because she is a very private person who I love and respect very much and do not wish to impose on her privacy. DeAnne is a woman of great strength(weather she knows it or not) and has such a great love for our Lord and for those who are lost and in prison. I believe that God has something great in store for her and that she will shine as she does her work for his glory.   DeAnne has overcome so much in the last couple of years and has learned a lot. But, she also knows that God NEVER gives us more than we can handle and that Everything happens for a reason. It has been an honor and a pleasure to be counted among her friends and we have shared both happiness and tears and good times and bad. Tina, DeAnne, Merry and I are all friends and I truly believe that God has something in mind for the four of us together. She has met both my daughter and my sister and was very kind to both of them! I love and respect you so much DeAnne and I have enjoyed knowing you more than you will ever know. You have done so much for so many and mark my words dear friend, God is not done with you yet!!!

Celebrating my birthday on one of our "Girl's Day". Who says being a Christian isn't fun?

DeAnne and her mother, Doris, who is also a spiritual powerhouse! Taken in 2018.

My sisters in Christ and I enjoying a sisters day out!

My three friends and I formed a sisterhood through Christ! One day we were at the fair I think, and we were saying that we should come up with a name for our little group. So, that night I was looking at stuff online and I saw some of the cutest pictures of some baby chics. I sent my friends the picture of the chics and funny as it is, there were exactly 4 chics that were

different colors and so cute. So each of us chose one of the chics to be our chic. I am not sure which one of us came up with the " 4 Christ " part of our name, but we all loved the idea and thus began calling ourselves Sister Chic's 4 Christ. Then one day out of the blue I decided to have some shirts and hats made for us. I went to a place that did t-shirt screening and I told them that I wanted to have four shirts made with our group name on it in the back and with a cross under our group name and that I wanted our first names put on the front. I then went to WalMart and purchased 4 black caps. Our sister Tina being the clothes designer, put rhinestones around the cross and she put crosses on the caps. When time and events allow, we have a sister's day out and we go see movies, go to spa's and go window shopping or go get something to eat or we go to some church even or even into prison to speak to women and show them that if we can change then they too can change! ANYTHING IS POSSIBLE THROUGH CHRIST!

The name of our Sisterhood in Christ is" Sister Chicks 4 Christ"

Sisters having fun together on a girl's day out

We all love oneanother very much and we would love to be able to spend more time together. I truly believe that God has a special plan for the four of us as I do not believe that our coming together was an accident nor is it an accident that we have formed a strong bond with oneanother!

Trying on hats at the State Fair.

My sister Tina and I on the day that I was presented with an award from parole. I am wearing a skirt she made for me! As always, my sister Tina agreed to share this special day with me and it meant so much to me!

Me enjoying myself at a church event.

The Sister Chic's at a church event enjoying ourselves! We had so much fun at this and every event that we are blessed enough to attend together!

Poems that I wrote for my friends The Sister Chicks

Merry

I have a friend whose name is Merry and she is the best
She has helped me through so much and many times she has put my mind to rest
She has been by my side for a few years now
She is a great source of strength and she has shown me that we will make it somehow

In the last few years she has been there through the smiles and the frowns
She has been there to help me celebrate the ups and to help me through the downs
She is beautiful, smart charismatic and so full of fun
She faces her trials with her head held high knowing that the Lord's will, will be done

I will always be thankful for her love and friendship and her smiles too
Because if it wasn't for her there were times I don't know what I would do
Merry, you will always be a special part of my life, never doubt how special you are to me
and on the day that daddy comes to take us away I know you will be among those who I will see…

Tina

I have an awesome friend whose name is Tina and she is full of talent and so much more
She and I had met in prison but our friendship has grown and she is someone who I truly adore
She is a seamstress, a poet and now she is an author and show host too
With God in her life, she knows there is nothing she can't do
She opens her heart and her home to so many who need a helping hand
And if you start feeling like your going to spiral out of control she will reach out and help yYou stand
Tina, you are special to me and will always have a special place in my heart
Together we will grow stronger and nothing will ever pull us apart…

DeAnne

You are a very special lady and you have come a very long ways
Lord only knows that you have had lonely nights and extremely long days
You have suffered through so much loss, but you have also had a lot of gain
I have seen you as you have taught others about God with a smile on your face and I have seen your
face full of pain
I want you to know that you have become so special to Tina, Merry and I in so many ways
And I look forward to sharing the future with the three of you as we share Gods love and
Sing his praise…

Ministry

My Church

Since my release from prison, I have been going to the Rosen Heights Baptist Church on the Northside of Fort Worth! My pastor Inavi Jimo and his beautiful wife Florence have helped us beyond words as has all of the congergation of my home church! When our house burned down they were there for us and helped us more than anyone could ever expect them to. Pastor Inavi did me the honor of Baptizing me in our church and was also very kind to my sister when she went to church with us.

I am very proud to be a part of Rosen Heights Baptist church and I love all of the wonderful missionary work they do and the tremendous outreach to the community and I love the fact that they accepted me as I am and did not react badly when I told them that I am a felon. I walked into Rosen Heights Baptist Church fresh out of prison. Because I had commited myself to keeping strong in my faith once I was released from prison, I immediately began a search for a home church. At first the reason I had chosen this particular church is because I only lived a couple of blocks away from the church and I figured that even if the weather was real bad I could walk to church and I did not have the excuse that I did not have a way to get there every week as even if my car did not have gas to go anywhere I was within walking distance.

When I first attended the church it had a different pastor. When Inavi was voted in as new pastor, you could immediately tell that he was more hands on then the other pastor was and he went to the hospital to visit people from our church when they are sick. You could tell and still can tell, that he loves being a pastor at our church and he truly loves the people of his church and he has a passion for the Lord that can be heard in his voice every Sunday!!! I had asked the pastor who was there before about getting baptized and he kept putting me off, pastor Inavi on the other hand got it done almost immediately after I spoke to him about it! They make you feel welcome from the moment you walk into the door and they sincerely love the people of the church and they know each of us by name as well as face. I can call my pastor any time for anything and if there is something that they can help me with (or anyone with) they will do it! Thank you Pastor Inavi, Florence and all of my Rosen Heights Church family for all of your love! I have been at this church now going on 5 years and I can not imagine ever going anywhere else!

My Discipleship Unlimited and Reignite Family

At the end of my time in prison I was on the Hobby Unit and I was put in a faith-based dorm as they said that they did not have anywhere else to put me. It was considered "over flow" but I don't believe in accidents! This dorm was ran by Discipleship Unlimited Ministries and its founder Linda Strom. There were so many wonderful, kind and patient volunteers who taught us about God, love, responsibility and so much more.

Discipleship Unlimited started an event called Reignite that is a reunion of those of us who graduated from the faith-based dorms in TDCJ where we all gather together for three days in April of every year and do praise and worship and we talk about what has happened in our lives since we saw each other the year before and we give praise reports about what God has done in our lives. The awesome men and women who had the heart to volunteer to teach us of God and his love are also there and some of us take a family member or friend to show them how awesome our Reignite Reunion is!

Below you can see some photos of Linda Strom, her son Terry Strom and his lovely wife Jean Strom who are all part of this awesome ministry and who all have the love of the Lord in their hearts. You will see pictures of Carla Hooton who ran the faith-based dorm on the Hobby Unit and who is an AWESOME woman who loves the Lord with all her heart! Her awesome husband Randy (May he rest in peace) was considered a father to many of us ladies in the faith-based dorm as I am sure he was a father figure at the men's units as well. We all miss Randy Hooton very much and I can't wait to see him in heaven one day. He was a gentle and loving man and you could see God shine through him. Their son Brady is doing missionary work and volunteered in the faith base dorm. We all love you Brady…

There is no way of telling how many souls have been changed or how many lives have been saved because of all the hard work and love that Linda Strom, Carla Hooton and many others have invested in those of us who were lost before going into the faith base dorms. Below you will also see some pictures of some of my Reignite family, me and my dear friend Tina Washington and many more of the lives that were changed through Christ. While in the faith base dorm, I was forced to face my past and to reconcile it.

It was the first time in my life that I finally felt free of my past and I felt like a totally new person. Truly I was, as I was a new creation in Christ!!! If I had not been put in that dorm I have no doubt that either I would be dead right now or back to doing drugs or yes, even back in prison. I thank God that I am not the person that I used to be anymore and now it is important to me to give back what I got from the faith base dorm, so I go into prisons and other facilities every chance that I get so that I can try to encourage those who are still lost to change their lives by showing them that if I a 30 year addict who had been to prison 4 times can change then so can they. Just give the Lord a chance and your possibilities are endless. I thank God for delivering me from my past and from my addiction as it was possible only through him!

The Strom Family

Brady, Carla, Linda, Me, Sue, Tina, Jacque

Me with Terry Strom

The Strom Family

Me speaking in an outfit designed and made by Tina.

Linda and I

Nellie Lisenby and I

The best volunteers ever!

Jean and I

This is George and Tina at the Reignite Reunion the year before last! Reignite comes once a year and is where a bunch of people who were in the Faith Based Dorms in TDCJ all over the state of Texas and all of the volunteers who walked us through our journey with much love and patience get together and talk about what God has done to change our lives and what we have done in our lives since our release from prison. It is where our faith family come together for 3 days and do a lot of praise and worship and catch up and do a lot of fun things together. I look forward to Reignite every April!

Tina and George at Reignite

Acting silly with Dino and
Merry who were also
in the faith-based dorms.

MY POEMS

MOM

It has been two year since you died and when I heard the news I cried.

I was glad that you were no longer in pain, don't get me wrong,

But we had allowed anger and bitterness to keep us apart far too long.

The mistakes that I made with you, my youngest children now make with me.

I beg them, please can't you just let go of the past... just let it be?

There are lots of time that I wish you were still here so we could have a fresh start,

That you could comfort me when my youngest children are breaking my tender heart.

But then I see how this world is soon going to be,

I am thankful that you're with God and not here with me.

Mom, I made a promise to you that I would never go back to drugs the last time we saw one another

And I am sure that you know that I've kept my promise to you my darling Mother.

So, rest in peace my darling mother knowing that I am more than okay.

And mom, I can't wait to see you again one day.

PRISONS

There are prisons which the state has designed

Then there are prisons that are of our hearts and of the mind.

The state-made prison can be escaped, or you can be let go.

But the mental prison you can't escape, it follows you everywhere you go.

The state-made prison is something that you can eventually get past.

The mental prison seems to never go away, how long will it last?

VALENTINES

Valentines, candy and balloons are symbols of the love we share

A beautiful way to show how much we care

Love is so fragile and beautiful at the same time

It endures hardships and makes your world shine

Nothing compares to the way love makes you feel

Time and love are the only two things that makes you heal

It gives you strength, courage and so much more

Nurture it, and share it with those you adore

Enjoy love and the way it makes your world shine

That is the meaning of love my valentine…

I LOVE

I love horses and the way it makes me feel when I ride
I feel so free with a feeling of peace deep inside
I love being in the country where no destruction or violence can be found
It's so peaceful where only natures songs can be heard for miles around
I love the feeling of freedom and God's beauty that can be seen everywhere
You can't find society's problems or all the pollution of the city there
If you want to go to a paradise like this and see God's beauty
there is only one place to go and that is the country

SWEETNESS

A piece of chocolate that melts in your mouth, oh so sweet
And if you add a strawberry, it makes such a wonderful treat.
A romantic walk with the one you love in the moonlight;
Sharing a sweet kiss under the stars makes everything just right.
What could possibly be better than a night like this?
A perfect night with your only love and a magical kiss.

WHAT I LOVE

I love to walk through the park on a beautiful summer day
And I love to listen to the children laugh and play
I love having a picnic in the shade of an oak tree
I love lying down on a blanket as the sun shines down on me
I love looking at all of the beautiful flowers growing all around
I love watching the children playing on the playground.
But most of all I love life and living in a country that is free
A place where I can go wherever I want and be whatever I want to be

OUR FUTURE

Our children are truly our future, don't you know
We don't want to watch them die but grow
We don't want them to grow up to become gang members or inmates
We don't want them to grow up behind ugly prison gates
So please watch your children as they grow
For they truly are our future, don't you know

A MOTHER'S PRAYER

God, I have always heard that you hear a mother's prayers.

You hear our prayers to protect our children from Satan and his snares.
You know the pain I feel for the loss of my mother;
You know the pain I feel being separated from RaeRae, her sister and brother.
So now I pray to you my heavenly father up above…
Grant to me my children's desire to give me their love.

I AM

I am the clown with balloons that make kids squeal with delight
I am the little teddy bear a child needs to be able to sleep at night
I am the cartoon on TV that puts a smile on a child's face
I am the beautiful dream that carries a child to that magical place
But mostly I am whatever a child needs me to be
Whatever makes them feel happy and safe
That is what I want to be

HOW CAN YOU BELIEVE

People have asked me how I can believe in God,
something that I cannot see,
And this was the answer that they got from me…
It's like the wind that blows through the trees
as though they were dancing;
Or like the fields of flowers
as if God knew the pleasure that they would bring.
Look at the birds that fly so freely in the sky,
so light and free;
Or how about all of the stars in the sky
and all of their beauty…
Even the moon that shines so beautiful
that seems to mesmerize.
So, when you hear that I believe in God…
Is it really any surprise?!

911

The pain and the loss as the planes hit the Twin Towers
The dead parents and children - yours, mine, and all of ours
The bravery of the passengers who overtook the terrorists
as they knew their lives would soon end
It was the rest of the innocent people

who these passengers were determined to save and defend
Terrorists are cowards who are brainwashed
to believe they are doing is right
Their own children are trained when they are young
to kill and to fight
All of the racial hate… the war against our people in uniform
It's no different than how terrorist are trained to do what they do
Hate, war and aggression towards others
it's all a learned behavior don't you know
We must change our ways if we are going to live
to watch our children grow
Our children must learn that all lives matter
no matter what the race or the job that they hold
Your children must be taught a better way to live
they must be told

FROM THE START
From a child who had been abused and mistreated all of her life
To an adult who lived in sadness with much strife
Going from being all alone without acceptance or love and not wanting to live
To someone who learned to overcome the past and learned how to forgive
There didn't seem to be any hope for a better future
How can she go on, what else will she have to endure
But then someone brought God into her life and showed her there was hope
They showed the way to live and love and they gave her the skills to cope

THE LIFE OF A CHILD
What is the life of a child, how is it supposed to be?
Isn't it supposed to be full of love and laughter? Can someone please tell me?
A child should not have to live a life of anger and bitterness or taught to live in fear.
Their lives should start out being pure, full of happiness and cheer.
I always wondered what a normal childhood is supposed to be like in a normal family.
Because the childhood I lived was full of sadness and I was always so lonely!

LOST
I started out being a child abused and all alone
I felt worthless, and unloved even after I was full grown
I lived a life full of drugs and sadness and of crime

I went from going to a shelter home to jail and finally doing prison time
I never thought I had a chance, and I didn't think there was hope for me
I did not understand God or what his plan could possibly be
I carried so much hatred and anger inside of me
I did not understand that letting it go would set me free

OUR SOLDIERS
Our American soldiers have stood strong by our country's side
They have defended our country with so much love and pride
I am sure that if Lady Liberty could she would already have shed many tears
For the loss of so many American Soldiers who fought for our freedom over the years
Over and over again our soldiers have kicked our enemies ass
Whether the fight was for our freedom or oil and gas
When it comes down to it, it doesn't matter why we kicked their asses so many times
All that matters is they tried to steal what was ours so now must pay for their crimes

ALL THE THINGS I DID TO MY FAMILY
I know that all of the things that I did to my family were wrong
And my heart sings to me a sad song
I sometimes wonder if I will always be all alone
And if I will be a person with a heart of stone
I used to be a person full of happiness and charm
That is until I stuck a needle in my arm
So, before you go sticking a needle in your arm
Thinking that it couldn't possibly cause so much harm
Please, stop and look at all of my mistakes
And save yourself a whole lot of heartaches

HELLO
Hello, my name is Mary and I am an addict who is lost and all alone
The life of drugs and crime is all that I have ever known
I'm broken and hurting deep inside as I have been for so many years
I've hurt a lot of people and I have caused so many tears
There are so many people like me who are lost and looking for peace
They are so full of anger and hatred which they don't know how to release
They have been lost for so long that they don't know which way to go
Doing drugs and time and running away are all that they know
Just know and remember that God is good and He really does love you

Turning your love, heart and life over to the Lord is all you have to do

MY REALITY

I was a horrible mother, a bad person and I sucked as a housewife
I got everything that I expected which wasn't much the way I was living my life
I was a great drug addict but at all else I was really very bad
But to be fair about it, look at the tragic childhood that I had
How could I be a good parent or teach my children well when I had nothing to go by
My father taught me that I would never succeed at anything no matter how hard I try
I wanted to be there with my children, wanted them to know they were loved and how much I care
But so many people betrayed me because they didn't want me there
My children were my last hope, they could have been the road to my salvation
I have had a lot of regrets in in my life, but none of them included my children

MY CHILDREN

A daughter who hates you so much that she wants to cause you more tears
She is in so much pain because her mother wasn't there for so many years
A grown son who in reality is just a lost little boy
He has survived so much abuse and pain, and has known so little joy
What is a mother to do about the children who are lost to her
How long will they be lost to her, how much more will she have to endure
Lord, please heal them of their pain and rid them of their sorrow
Please Lord, let them realize time is so short and it's something we can only borrow

THE 911 MASSACRE

My heart goes out to all of those who lost a loved one in the 911 massacre
I know it's something you will never forget and something almost impossible to endure
I can't imagine how those people must have felt as they saw their lives flash before their eyes
The fear as the Twin Towers fell to the ground and the planes fell from the skies
There were so many senseless deaths on that horrible, tragic day
I saw it on the news and those images will never go away
There were many losses that fateful day, but there were many heroes as well
The ones who overtook the terrorists on one plane
and those who dug out our dead after the Twin Towers fell
The sadness, the fear and the loss that came with 911 will always be in our memories
And I pray to God that there will never again be a repeat of these tragedies

MY FANTASY WORLD

I have a fantasy world that I wish could be for real

A world where you don't have to live in fear, and you can share how you feel.

In my fantasy world, there are children laughing and playing all the time.

They can play without fear, as in my fantasy world there is no violence or crime.

In my fantasy world, people treat animals and each other with respect and love.

In my fantasy world, there is still prayer in schools; purity is symbolized by a dove.

In my fantasy world, men don't have to be soldiers; there is no such thing as war.

In my fantasy world, families spend quality time together because there are no computers, video games or TV anymore.

In my fantasy world, there are no abusive parents, hungry and homeless people, and no drug or alcohol addiction.

In my fantasy world, everyone lives together in peace whether black, white or Hispanic... everyone.

In my fantasy world, no one must worry about money and bills or how they will survive.

In my fantasy world, people help one another and that's how they stay alive.

In my fantasy world, there is no need for police or jail or prisons, none of that.

I know, I know, it's not practical, but it's my fantasy world - where I wish I was.

A DREAM WORLD

Sometimes I wonder what this world would be like if it were a perfect place

With beautiful flowers growing everywhere and everyone with a smile on their face

Birds singing beautiful songs as they fly around in the sky

Children laughing and playing and waving as they go by

Families spending time together and enjoying life as it used to be once upon a time

When there were no divorces, terrorists, or so much crime

Being able to walk around without a worry in the world and a smile on our face

Wouldn't that be so awesome, wouldn't it be such a wonderful place?

OH, MY DARLING CHILD

Oh, my darling child, how I truly love you.

It sometimes amazes me to see the things you do Oh my darling child,

you are so dear to me.

I can't wait to see what you will grow up to be.

Oh my darling child, remember there is not " anything " you ca.n't do,

And no matter what happens, I'll always be here for you

Oh, my darling child, I wish you could always be innocent and carefree.

But you know dear child of mine, no matter what, you'll always be a baby to me.

CHILD OF GOD
You're a child of God who is so full of his glory that your filled with great beauty
And I want to thank you for choosing to become a friend and mentor to me Joyce,
you are so sweet, caring and so very kind
You are the kind of friend everyone hopes to one day find
So, let me once again thank you for your friendship and TLC
And a great big thank you for the prayers you send to heaven for me…

I WALKED YOU THROUGH
I walked you through my childhood that was full of fear and feeling all alone
Then I walked you through my teenage years feeling unloved but not yet full grown
I told you about growing up being unloved by my mother and my father
I walked you through all of the pain and suffering which I had to endure
Now I will tell you about my life and how it was as an adult
It really wasn't much different, I had to endure injuries and a lot of insult
But then one day I was taught about God and his undying love for me
When I was taught about God and his undying love for me
of my past I was finally set free

MY SON
I have always wished the very best in life for you my son
I am proud that you graduated high school and the other things you've done
I am so sorry for all the hard things you have gone through in your life
You have been through so much sadness, been through many changes and strife
I know you will win over this battle of addiction my darling son
Want to wish you a happy birthday and pray next year it will be a better one

MY DAUGHTER RAE RAE
Though my daughter Rae Rae and I are close in miles, we are still far apart
This is not the way I imagined the beginning being, but it's a start
I prayed so long that she would come back into my life and accept me as her mother
I have dreamt of all of us being together one day - she and I, her sister and brother
I wish she could see how much I have missed and loved her throughout the years
I want to truly be her mother and to become her friend
I want her to know that upon me she can truly depend

THE SCRIPTURES SAY
If you'll look at Psalm 116, you'll see how much God truly does care

And when you read the armor of God, it will arm you against evil and help you to prepare

No matter where you look in The Bible, there is something to learn

Like the fact that salvation is God's gift to us and not something we can earn

If you will read Ecclesiastes 3:1-8, you will learn that for everything under Heaven there is a season

And in Matthew 6:9, you will learn to pray for His will to be done

There are many warnings against sin such as murder, bearing false witness and greed

Our lessons begin in Genesis all the way to Revelation and you better take heed

A PRAYER FOR MY CHILDREN

Dear Heavenly Father, I pray my children's souls for you to always keep

And protect them as they lay their heads down to sleep

Forgive them for the way they treat me for they know not what they do

Lord, I pray when this sinful world comes to an end, my children will belong to you

I wasn't there for them, I didn't help them when they fell

Lord you know they suffered, you know they went through hell

Let someone lead them to you father, and show them the way

Lead them down the right path my Lord

So, they can be with you come judgement day

It breaks my heart to see how my youngest children have chosen to live

I pray that you show them mercy and let them learn to forgive

Please let them open their eyes get to know you before it's too late

You will give them a clean slate

FALSE HOPE

The way that you were taken from me was so cruel and unfair

You thought that I had run out on you and that I didn't care

I was so scared and nervous as I went to meet you

the daughter I had not seen in 10 years

I was so happy and full of hope as I reached out to hug you with my eyes full of tears

Neither one of us knew how to act, what to think or even what to do

All I knew for sure, was that my dreams were finally coming true

I could not believe that you had been told that I had died 10 years before

At first you seemed to be happy to meet me, that was until I walked out the door

Something happened after we met that first night that changed you

Someone turned you against me, how easy it was for them to do

You have always thought that I had walked out on you

but the truth is that you were taken away from me

You asked me what happened, but you don't want the truth
it's something you don't want to see
You say that I hurt you and you say that I caused you so much pain
The games you have been playing with my heart and my mind are driving me insane
Darling daughter, the past has nothing to offer us, it can't do any good
Can't you understand my dear, I would change the past if I could

SO MUCH PAIN
My darling child, you have absolutely no idea what I have gone through
You have no idea how much it hurt me when I lost you
My darling child, you only think you know the meaning of real pain
First the loss of my son and then losing you too, it drove me insane
I lost control and I did not care about anything anymore
I have been through so much in my life I have even been through this before
Your brother's father took him from me when he was only two months of age
Oh how hurt I was, there was no justice, it was an outrage
Then I gave up your sister because my mother drove me insane
The way I was mistreated by my mother and Robert was inhumane
James took you away from me when you were five, and I thought I would die
He took you because his nephew said I asked for drugs, but it was a lie
Whether you believe it or not my darling child,
for 10 years I searched for you high and low
I searched everywhere until I had no place else to go
My darling child, I pray you never have to know the pain of losing your child
as it is a deep pain
There is nothing like that pain child of mine, it can drive you insane
You have been poisoned against me from the very start
And the way you have treated me is breaking my heart

MY LOST SON
Oh, darling son of mine, it hurts me to see how you chose to live
The pain that you won't let go of and the inability to forgive
I know you're hurting a lot and trust me, I know your pain is great
But, my darling son, you don't have to let that pain seal your fate
You have tried so hard to cause me pain and to hurt me in a specific way

THE DEDICATED DAUGHTER
Oh, my darling daughter, you are so special to me and so close to my heart

I am so thankful that my addiction and my past didn't tear us apart

I am so thankful that you don't hate me or

want to hurt me the way my other children do

The price of my past has been so high, and I have lost so much

but thankfully I still have you

You have been a great source of encouragement to me my sweet Mary,

And I thank you for never losing hope or giving up on me

Mary, your love and encouragement and your faith in me gives me the strength

to fight the battle that I struggle with from within

Because of that my darling child, I have no doubt

that I will never go back to my old way of life again

I love you so much my darling dedicated daughter

and not getting to see more of you just breaks my heart

It doesn't seem fair that the only child who loves me

and I must live so many miles apart

I pray that one day we will be able to live closer to one another

You and I, and who knows, maybe even your sister and brother

MY TESTIMONY

When I was 8 years old, my future didn't seem very bright I didn't know about God,

so, my life was as dark as night

There was nothing but pain and loneliness throughout each day

And I didn't have anyone to how me the right way

By the time I was 13, I was putting a needle in my arm

After all, my friends and peers assured me it was okay,

it couldn't cause any harm

By the time I became a legal adult, I was given my first sentence to a prison

You see, I had to pay the price for the bad things that I had done

But, don't think just because I went to prison that I was done

No way, I was grown now, and I could have a lot more fun

I didn't realize that God had my back, he had been by my side along the way,

He was patiently waiting for me to ask for his help and learn to obey

You see, God gives us the freedom of choice,

our way of living is whatever we choose,

So, did I follow God and his guiding light,

or did I go down the same path where all I could do is lose

Well I decided I hadn't had enough fun yet, I wasn't quite done

And now, I'm doing my third sentence in this state prison

I finally realized how tired I was, and I got on my knees

With tears running down my face, I asked God "forgive me, won't you please

I asked God into my heart and I accepted him as my Lord and savior

And the Lord has made my life and it's trials a lot easier to endure

God says there is nothing he won't forgive if you ask it in his name

He does not judge your past and he does not want you to be full of shame

You are his child and he loves you, my dear friend

With God in your life, all of the darkness and pain will end

So, invite God into your heart and accept him as your Lord and savior,
won't you please

That's all you must do, then just bow your head in prayer and on bended knees

GOODBYE TO YOU

This is a letter to that hypnotic drug called speed

For a long time you were my only desire, my need

I used you up my nose, in a pipe and finally in my arm

When I used you I had no thoughts or care about who I would harm

Now I have something to tell you and you better listen well

I am through with you and you can go straight to hell

I have God in my life now, and I no longer feel the need to get high

You see, God delivered me from you, so this is goodbye

Also, you think you destroyed my life and stole my family

But that's a lie, because God will restore both back to me

I've got to hand it to you, you had a hold on me for many years

You played with my mind, broke my family's hearts and caused many tears

But God fought you for me and he won the war

For the first time in my life I know I don't have to live like that anymore

EPILOGUE

I have written this book in honor of those who have had an impact on my life. I did not put these in a special order as not to offend anyone, as everyone mentioned in this book are important to me, and I do not want anyone to think the other people are more important to me than they are. Each person is special in their unique way.

God has placed many special people in my life since He delivered me from my addiction, and I am so thankful for each one of you! I never thought that I would have such awesome people in my life, nonetheless so many! It is an awesome feeling to know that I am so loved.

I guess this book is my way to say thank you to those of you who have been with me through both the good and the bad and the hard times, as well as the easy times. I am in awe of all of you and the many things that I have learned from you. My father told me at a young age that I would not be loved by anyone and that basically I was worthless, but all of you are the proof that he was wrong.

First and foremost, of course, I owe my thanks to God for strategically placing each of you on my path in and on my journey. Through each of you, I have learned valuable lessons and I have grown both as a woman and as a person. I value each person who is in my life and am grateful for having had them in my life!

I hope that all of you will enjoy this book and know that I say everything from the bottom of my heart! May God bless each and every one of you and your families now and always!

THE END

Made in the USA
Middletown, DE
31 March 2021